My Blue Heaven

Best Wishes
to Carl & Cathy

H L Arsenault

My Blue Heaven

From Charles Lindbergh to
John F. Kennedy

H. George Arsenault

Writers Club Press
San Jose New York Lincoln Shanghai

My Blue Heaven
From Charles Lindbergh to John F. Kennedy

Writers Club Press
an imprint of iUniverse.com, Inc.

For information address:
iUniverse.com, Inc.
5220 S 16th, Ste. 200
Lincoln, NE 68512
www.iuniverse.com

ISBN: 0-595-20017-6

Printed in the United States of America

Dedication

This book is dedicated to Margaret Elizabeth Foley, my loving wife of twelve years, and my seven children, Mary Ann, Patrick Joseph, Margaret Elizabeth, Robert Ernest, Mark Anthony, Aileen Therese, and Janet Frances, for their unfailing love and support before and after their mother died on May 26, 1964.

Preface

Much like the Shakespearean tragedy, Hamlet, tells the story of how fate, *with the slings and arrows of outrageous fortune*, deals a man a devastating blow, destroying his status quo, and how he confronts it. *My Blue Heaven* is a true story of like manner. In the *preface* of my first published book *One Plus One Equals Nineteen*, I mentioned this paradox.

I discovered that blue can not only mean happiness, like *blue skies* or the *blue bird of happiness* or *blue bird hill* as in the movie *Going My Way*, but sometimes it can also mean sadness, similar to *singing the blues* in our jazz age. How to cope with these events that fate presents us with from time to time is something that every one of us must learn in order to avoid chronic depression. Searching for answers, I turned to the bible with its reference to faith, hope and charity. Reading the philosophical wisdom of sages of the past, I found the support I needed. I learned I could pray for faith and always have hope for charity. I became an optimist.

Therefore, I have always alleged to be an optimist. I remember reading this axiom: *as you wander on through life, whatever is your goal, keep your eye upon the doughnut and not upon the hole.*—This became my motto. *The glass isn't half empty—it's half full!*

Acknowledgments

The renowned mystery writer, William X. Kienzle, who has written at over twenty mystery novels, including the *Rosary Murders* that was made into a movie of the same name, is an old Holy Redeemer School classmate of mine. Bill's wife, Javan, a retired proofreader and editor from the Detroit Free Press, reviewed my original manuscript, which was written into two major parts combined and called *Seven Come Eleven* as one manuscript. As you may have read in my prior book, *One Plus One Equals Nineteen*, I was fortunate to obtain their astute counseling.

Javan read my manuscript and made many corrections suggesting that I really had two books. It became clear to me, that because of the total distinction and uniqueness of the two parts, I really had two stories that could not be told together as one book. Bill and Javan encouraged me to pursue its publication. Neal Shine, retired publisher of the Detroit Free Press and one of Michigan's most respected journalists, who is a neighbor of mine, also encouraged me to publish this autobiography.

Having been rejected by many publishers and at Bill Kienzle's suggestion, I solicited Berl Falbaum, an author and professional public relations specialist, former reporter for The Detroit News, teacher at two state universities, to assist me in the final proof reading of my manuscript in preparation for self publication. Berl suggested that I concentrate on seventeen and thus, *One Plus One Equals Nineteen* preceded book I. That book is a happy lighthearted chronicle that tells the story of how one widow and one widower merged in a joint venture of marriage to raise seventeen children. It relates all the problems and how they were solved. Now, My Blue Heaven is the beginning or what came before that story.

I especially wish to acknowledge my debt to Delores Ann Shmina McMillan Arsenault, my wife of "1+1=19," for her devoted love and support in helping me with my writing efforts, by proofreading, critiquing, and correcting both books: *One Plus One Equals Nineteen* and now, *My Blue Heaven.*

Introduction

Ulysses S. Grant in the preface of his **Personal Memoirs of U.S. Grant** stated, *"Man proposes and God disposes."* I have the same opinion. There are many important events in our lives that are not in our plans nor brought about by their own choice. God or fate has a way of writing our history in such a manner that seems to go beyond our thoughts and expectations. Sometimes the events in our lives exceed the best fiction or prophecy of anyone's imagination. So it was in my day.

I

My Philosophy

There are more things in heaven and earth, Horatio,
Than are dreamed of in your philosophy.—Shakespeare.

"What's your philosophy for life?" A certain professor of philosophy was asking us. "Your homework is to write a short paper stating your philosophy for life. Something simple," he said, "that would identify what you believe and what were your rules and values for living the good life." I remember that that 'short paper' was not simple but a rather difficult task.

Socrates talked about "defining your terms" before he could discuss anything. We need to know what is meant by *philosophy* before we can write our *philosophy for life*. Socrates defined *philosophy* as the pursuit of wisdom and one who seeks knowledge or a seeker of the truth. Webster defines *philosophy of life* as "…an attitude towards life and the purpose of life." With this, I attempted to define my most general beliefs, concepts, and attitudes for my life in the following dissertation.

From my youth, I always wanted to live honorably. I felt that a person who lives honorably would never cheat, never lie, never steal, and never waiver from the straight and narrow path of fairness. He will know the difference between right and wrong and always choose right. His reward will be a good life and eternal happiness. I thought of myself as a knight in shining armor, riding a white horse and ready to slay the evil dragon for his beautiful princess. The dragon was sin and therefore, like Tom Sawyer told his aunt when she asked him what the preacher said about sin, he answered, "He's agin it!" *(Sic)* And so was I. This is my philosophy.

As time went on, I found that the challenge for me in later years was to pass this sense of moral purpose and values on to my children so, then, hopefully, they could enjoy the happiness and rewards of a life well spent. The feelings and problems that spiritual impoverishment can lead to depression and unrelenting sadness. This is something every one of us sometimes experience. I was taught at an early age to trust in God and never lose hope. I was happy that I had been given faith and could look to God for guidance, strength and support.

Without this philosophy and religion, I don't know how I could have faced the life that was waiting for me in the near future. I was told that nothing was impossible with the help and guidance of God and that one could easily attain the blue heaven of their dreams if they only had faith in God.

A Frenchman, named Antoine de Rivarol, over two hundred years ago stated, It *is easy for men to write and talk like philosophers, but to act with wisdom, there's the rub!* Wisdom—now—there's the rub! I remember starting to pray for wisdom when my father died. I was nine years old and wondered why my dad had died. I worried about my mother having enough money to continue living in our house. Luckily, my dad had paid cash for the house.

After my father died, the teaching nuns in my Catholic school told me to pray for the wisdom to understand God's plan. So, at nine years old, I added a prayer for wisdom every night before I went to bed. I thought that I could solve all my problems easily and successfully and the world would be mine if only God would grant me wisdom.

From the beginning, my mother taught my brother, sister and I to say our prayers on our knees every night before we went to bed. I remember that we would always include: "God bless mother, dad and my brother and sister, etc." With the etcetera, we would include a bunch of other people. At nine years old, as a third grader, I was still praying every night. In fact, we were taught to say night prayers and morning prayers. It was many years later that this practice changed. As I was growing up, in high school, I decided that you need not be on your knees to pray and you don't have to wait for bedtime or morning.

II

In The Beginning

The Book of Life begins with a man and woman in a garden.
It ends with Revelations.—Oscar Wilde.

The year was 1671 when Pierre, a navigator on a French sailing ship called "L'Oranger" sailed out of La Rochelle, France and headed west for the new world. He was the first Arsenault to arrive in the North American continent. Born in 1650, at Rochefort, a small village near the central west coast of France. Pierre, at the age of 21, landed at Port Royal, Acadia in what is now called Nova Scotia, Canada.

Nine generations later, on the 30th of September 1927, I was born. This was the month that Charles Lindbergh first published his new book recounting his solo flight over the Atlantic of the prior May when Paris had hailed him the *Lone Eagle*. He called his book "We" because— as he stated in his book—his lonely flight could not have happen without the support of many associates

It was a good year. The stock market was rising higher and higher, making more and more of its speculators rich. Babe Ruth set a new record with his 60th home run of the season and the Yankees beat the Pirates for the World Series. The first talking picture, *The Jazz Singer* starring Al Jolson, was released.

The *Teapot Dome scandal* caused the Supreme Court to rule that the Navy oil land leases in Wyoming were invalid. The developing automotive industry was creating a new middle class society. The song of the day was *I'm Looking Over A Four Leaf Clover.* This truly was "…a brave new world" as Aldous Leonard Huxley had hypothesized and the dollar was king.

The Big Depression

Then came the depression in 1929. I knew nothing of the hardships of the depression that the world was facing in the thirties. I was growing up with no idea of the hard times the majority of people had finding work. My father was a barber and went to work every day, and we always had a good home with enough to eat. We lived only a block from the railroad tracks and I remember, many times, hobos knocking on our back door and asking for something to eat. My mother always gave them a sandwich. I remember over hearing my dad and uncles talking about someone *getting the broom or being fired.* I wondered why they were given a broom, and how does one get fired without being burnt. I remember how one of my mother's cousins, uncle John, use to give my brother and I a penny every time he came over to our house and how those pennies stopped when he was out of work.

Detroit

I grew up in Detroit's Southwest side. I had two older brothers and two younger sisters. My oldest brother, Robert, was born in 1924. He was 'a blue baby' and died in May of 1926. My other brother, Albert, was born August 25, 1926. My two younger sisters were Geraldine, born in 1929, and Martha, born in 1933. Geraldine died in 1931. I do not remember the death of my sister Geraldine. In those days, people who died were laid out in their home and a wreath of flowers was hung on the door to signify that someone had died. It was customary for a few relatives of the deceased to stay up all night with the body until the day of the funeral. The children would be sent to stay at a relative's home.

This was the beginning of my journey on the road of life that every one of us must travel. Happenings in our early environment influence us later as the dynamics of a changing world is reflected in our ability to learn right from wrong. What I learned in my youth influenced many of my future decisions—decisions that effected my future successes and failures.

Life is filled with making decisions. What happens tomorrow depends on what decisions we make today. I thought if we make good decisions, good things will happen, and if we make bad decisions, bad things will happen. Even though sometimes with good decisions, bad things can happen. Yet, I felt I should strive to learn the wisdom of making only good and wise decisions—easier said than done.

A New Deal

The election of Franklin D. Roosevelt as President in 1934 and his "nothing to fear but fear itself" started to bring us out of the depression. In 1936, Social Security was enacted along with The National Labor Relations Act to help the "poor working man," and became part of FDR's New Deal. The times seemed to promise a better tomorrow for all, including our family, but in November of that year, my father died.

The day was November 4, 1936, when my dad came home from his barbershop in the middle of the day—not feeling well—he took a hot bath and went to bed. The next morning my dad felt worse so my mother called the doctor (those were the days when doctors made house calls.) The doctor treated him for the common cold or flu. But, the next day, my dad grew worse. On the fourth day, my dad's brother, Gus, called his doctor to come and see his brother, "Ernie." My dad's doctor was also there. After my uncle's doctor had examined my dad, we overheard the two doctors talking loudly behind closed doors. When they came out of the room, the doctor told us that my dad was dying. He had a burst appendix that had poisoned his system. It was too late to operate and the doctor said there was nothing they could do for him.

My dad, realizing his time was short, asked to see his children. My mother called us into the bedroom. I can still remember my dad's last words as we were brought to the side of his bed.

"Martha," he said to my three-year-old sister, "always stay as sweet as you are…" Then he turned to me.

"George," he said, "you be good!" I guess I was always testing everything and getting into trouble. But, I remember him saying to me "be good," and I remember thinking that I would be good. My dad then told my brother,

"Albert, you're the man of the house now. Take care of your mother."

Turning to my mother, he said, "Anna, sell the barber shop—keep the car and learn to drive."

After my father died, my mother rented two of our four upstairs bedrooms. First, her brother, uncle Bob and a bachelor cousin rented the rooms paying weekly, and later years "roomers" who worked at the nearby General Motors Ternstedt Plant rented the rooms. I remember my mother putting a "Rooms For Rent" sign in our front window and a picture of "Our Mother of Perpetual Help" next to it. Renting rooms was her only source of income. Somehow she managed to keep the family together and pay her bills. She was very good at budgeting and stretching the dollar to make ends meet. My brother and I got jobs selling magazines and later the Detroit News daily paper to try to help out.

Sometime after my dad died, someone gave us a spitz dog, and we named him Skippy. He was a happy dog and a friend of the whole neighborhood. Every day I would come home from school, I would whistle and call "Skippy!" He would come running out of nowhere to welcome me home. One day, when I called him, I saw him running from across the street right in front of a passing car. He was hit and the man stopped. He was a very nice man and said that he was sorry the dog ran in the street. It was right in front of our house on Military and my mother heard the screeching car as he tried to avoid hitting the dog and came running out to see what was the matter. The man asked me, "Is this your dog?"

"Yes," I said wiping my eyes, "his name's Skippy."

"I'm very sorry," he said. Then turning to my mother, he said, "are you this boys mother?"

"Yes."

"Would you like me to dispose of the dead dog?"

"Yes," she said, "if you will be so kind."

The man picked up the limp body of Skippy and gently put him in the trunk of his car and drove away.

These things I remember about my first real encounter with the death. These images, in later years, would come back to me in vivid memory.

III

School Days

Youth is the opportunity to do something and to become somebody.
T. T. Munger—1830-1910 (American Clergyman)

Three things happened in my youth that would benefit me in later years, as you will see. First, I spent two years in the second grade; second, I learned to tumble as a cheerleader in my sophomore and senior year of high school; and third, I accepted a chance to learn radio repair in my last two years of high school in a program the Catholic schools had with the Detroit Public schools.

I have concluded that what happens in one's life depends more on the individual's decisions rather than on what God directs. What happens tomorrow depends on what we do today. God gives us brains; He expects us to use them. He's not about to perform a miracle to save us if we are going to be stupid about it. God will help us on the way but we must make our own decisions and one decision is to ask for His help.

St. Thomas Aquinas said, "Pray as if everything depends on God, and work as if everything depends on you." But, God works in his own ways that we may find difficult to understand. Maybe God has special plans for all of us that we do not understand. And perhaps the happenings in my youth were designed to prepare me for a special job that God had planned for me in later years.

I also believe that if you love life and wish to see good days, then as the Bible says (Peter 3 verse 10), *For he that would love life and see good days, let him refrain his tongue from evil, and his lips that they speak no guile. Let him eschew evil, and do well—let him seek peace and ensue it.*

As I have said, I like to think that God rules my life and I have nothing to fear. From day one, my parents taught me to have faith in God. My mother had great faith and passed that on to her children. It has helped me travel through this journey in life and still keep my head when all about me are losing theirs. Life is a learning experience with all of its events. And we never stop learning through out our life.

Someone said, "You are what you eat." I think that we could add, you are what your early environment and training prepares and conditions you to be. I think we are a direct product of our early environment and experiences that influence our decisions in life. I felt it was important I make my decisions wisely if I wanted to amount to anything.

When I started school in 1933, I had a problem that I didn't know about. In the second grade, I was having trouble keeping up with reading and writing in English. Because my French parents wanted their children to be fluent in their native tongue, only French was spoken in our home. I was late in learning English. I could speak fluently in French but in the second grade, I was made fully aware of what I was lacking English when I was held back a year. I was expected to keep up with the other children who were five years ahead of me in use of the English language. It didn't bother me and I was not unhappy with this event. However, it would later prove to be very beneficial to me. I remember someone saying, "Learn to read and read books, and you'll never be lonely." I found out that there are books written on everything. Each book has at least one gem in them. Look for that piece of knowledge or gem and go on from there. As a teacher once advised when I was writing my thesis, "first find out what has been written on the subject, then take it one step further." Good advice.

After my dad died in 1936, my brother and I had part time jobs trying to help my mother. I sold the Liberty magazine, The Saturday Evening Post, The Ladies Home Journal and Physical Culture magazines. The magazine manager would deliver them to my home and I would find customers and pay him at the next delivery. The Liberty and Saturday Evening Post were five cents and the Ladies Home Journal was ten cents and the Physical Culture was a quarter. A barbershop was my only customer for the Physical Culture magazine. At the age of twelve, we got newspaper delivery routes for the Detroit News.

At age fifteen, I worked part time for a men's store, washing windows and helping in sales when they were busy. In my junior year, I got a job as an usher at the local Hollywood Theater. Because of my working after school, I was not able to tryout for any sports to earn a school letter. However, regimented practice was not so demanding for the cheerleaders, so, in my Junior year, I joined the Cheer Leading Squad to earn my school letter and became one of five cheer leaders—four Senior boys and one Junior—me.

The next year, my senior year, it was up to me to organize a cheer leading squad. I engaged my close friends, Don Schneider, Jack Brabenac, Melvin Kurpinski in my senior class and Tom Regan, our one junior.

There were five senior girls that wanted to be cheerleaders. And as captain of the Cheerleading squad, I talked to Mother Superior of the IHM nuns for her permission to let these five girls join our cheerleading squad. It would be the only chance for a high school girl to earn a school letter. This was a *first* in the parochial schools and the first time in Redeemer history. We had five girls and five boys. I found a book on tumbling at the local library and the boys all learned how to tumble for our new cheers.

In this last year of high school, our basketball team won a championship and our football team almost won the West Side championship losing only to Lourdes high school.

SOMETHING TO CHEER ABOUT

Those Holy Redeemer High basketball and football teams certainly have given the cheer leaders something to cheer about during the past few years. Redeemer surprised the prep football world with a sensational record in 1944 by taking the Parochial League title, defeating Catholic Central, and staging a grand stand against Mackenzie at the Goodfellow Grid Classic for a thrilling climax. The basketball team followed up with a championship. This year's football team turned in an excellent record, only losing the West Side championship to Lourdes at U. of D. Stadium two weeks ago.

The Redeemer cheer leaders shown above are from left to right, bottom row: Mary Barigian, Phyllis Hendrie, Betty McAuliffe, Teresa Rusalik and Joan Diroll. The boys in the top row from left to right are: Jack Brabenac, George Arsenault, Melvin Kurpinski, Don Schneider and Tommy Regan.

IV

The US Army

The best armor is to keep out of gunshot.
Francis Bacon 1561-1626

On September 30, 1945, the Second World War was still raging in the Pacific. I was eighteen (draft age), and just starting my senior year in high school. Luckily, the draft board gave this their consideration and I was able to get a deferment from the draft to finish my senior year. Had I not been held back in the second grade, I might have been drafted in June of 1945 and probably shipped out to the Pacific, prior to the war's end in August of 1945. I may have also missed my junior and senior years as a tumbling cheerleader as well as my two years studying radio repair at the Southfield Technical Training Center.

When I graduated from high school in June of 1946, I, with four of my friends, enlisted in the regular army. We knew we had to serve anyway. The Army advertisements were encouraging enlistments promising the "GI Bill." Every day on the radio we would hear that the army had forty thousand jobs that an enlistee could choose from in the regular Army. Also, they were accepting short-term enlistments of eighteen months. The draftees were still being inducted for the duration plus six months—whatever that meant. As an enlistee, I knew the exact date of my discharge—no duration to worry about. The radios kept saying, "Make it a million enlistees for the Army of Occupation and let the boys come home." I started my enlistment on October 1, 1946. My discharge date would be April 1, 1948.

The president of my senior class, Dick Telnack, wanted to enlist in the Navy but they were only taking four-year enlistments. They told him that the Marines across the hall were accepting enlistments for two years. So he became a Marine for two years. When he was discharged, he joined the Trappist Monks in Conyers, Georgia. He helped build a new monastery called The Monastery of the Holy Spirit. As an artist, he designed and built the stained glass windows of their church. He went on to design and build stain glass for churches all over the world. This became his contribution to the Trappist monks and to this day, he has continued his work at the monastery in Georgia.

Fort Sheraton, Chicago, Illinois

The army sent me and other new recruits and enlistees, to Fort Sheraton Chicago where we were given our uniforms and other clothing. We picked up a GI duffle bag, packed with all our issued fatigues, class A uniforms, shirts tie, hat, raincoat, socks, shorts and T shirts. We lugged this now heavy bag to the medical building where we got in line for some kind of shot. The guys coming out told us that they used square needles and some said that they had propellers on the end of the needles. This is where we received our first tetanus shot. With aching arms, we lugged our heavy duffle bag back to a barracks where we changed to our new uniforms. I had forty-four sized under shirts and I took about a thirty-six. Our pants were too long, but I guess that's why we were told to blouse them in our boots.

The next day, we were busy taking IQ tests and getting more shots. The following day, we were given our assignments for training. I was assigned to go to the anti-aircraft replacement training center at Fort

Bliss, Texas. About fifty of us were put on a train heading for Texas. We were seven days on that train because of bad weather, we were told. The diner car ran out of food on the third day, and we were given K rations. There were three kinds of rations. Breakfast, lunch, and dinner. We never knew which one we would be handed. We would trade if we didn't like what we received. The nice part about the K rations, is that they also included candy and cigarettes. Since I was not a smoker at that time, I trade the cigarettes for extra candy.

Fort Bliss, El Paso, Texas

When we arrived at the El Paso train station, it was about three o'clock in the morning. The temperature was about forty-five degrees and we were in our summer uniforms. It was cold standing on the station platform. Finally some trucks pulled up. A Sergeant jumped out of the truck and yelled, "Alright, lets get these men out of this hot sun." I'll never forget that because that was opposite what I was thinking.

At camp, we went into the mess hall and they served us hot coffee. I didn't drink coffee, so all I had was a glass of water. That was my introduction to Fort Bliss. I found myself assigned to Battery B of the 58th Anti Aircraft Battalion. We were being trained to fire, disassemble and reassemble the M1 rifle and an automatic sub machine gun, called the grease gun. This weapon was made with a stiff wire attached to what appeared to be a piece of pipe. We learned to shoot the grease gun in bursts of three because the gun would tend to climb upward and to the right as you fired it. The grease gun uses 45-caliber ammunition making it very lethal at close range.

Basic training was hectic for me, to say the least. I wondered if I'd ever get out of it. Would it ever be over? Every hour of every day, the army had us busy marching, running the obstacle course, attending lectures and doing calisthenics. There was many a night that I was assigned to do Guard Duty and many a day I was assigned to KP (kitchen police) duty. I found out that the battery clerk assigned guard duty and KP alphabetically. So, Arsenault was one of the first for both. (Incidentally, in the Army, they only used your last name. We got use to calling every-one by his last name.) When I was assigned KP and Guard Duty for the second time while some guys had not yet been assigned, I asked the our training Cadre, "why?" He said the battery clerk got mixed up on his list so he started the alphabet over. I'll bet there's a guy named Tom Zink somewhere who never had KP or Guard duty.

I found out that, in the army, the word *police* meant to pick up and clean up. When we were told to police the area, they didn't mean *guard duty,* they meant to clean up the area. We were told that if we saw something on the ground, pick it up. If we can't pick it up, paint it. And if it moved, salute it. I learned that every morning, you better check the bulletin board outside the mess hall for your name. It was here that we were told who was on KP and who was on guard duty, as well as other assignments.

It was during basic training that the army gave us more immuniza-tion shots for various diseases. There were many days when we were told to change to strip down to only raincoats and boots and they would march us to the medical buildings where we would stand in long lines waiting to enter a building. We were never told what was up. Many times they would give us a shot in the arm and on another occasion of raincoats and boots standing in line, was for a dental check up. It is dur-ing basic training that any dental work you might need was done. The army didn't bother asking you if you would like to have dental work, they told you. That's an order! Now I knew what was meant in the say-ing, "you never know where you're going until you get there." And, "hurry up and wait."

I had some cavities that needed attention. It seemed that every Monday, I was on the roster for the dentist. I would have rather have gone with my buddies, but in the Army they don't ask you what you want, they tell you. One thing I can say about the dental work the Army did for me was that I never had a tooth ache again.

The basic training was too regimented for my taste. Our days were detailed from morning to night. We did have Saturdays and Sundays off. There was a recreation room with pool tables, ping-pong and games. The autumn weather on the desert is hot every day and cold every night. To make matters worse, the wind, at night, would blow sand through the hut-vents. In the mornings we had sand all over the inside of our huts. We had to shake the sand out of our blankets and sweep the hut floors each day. Nighttime was my time! I was happy every night to be left alone in my bed, in our four man huts.

I remember one night a wild thunderstorm hit our huts in this desert. The wind howled and the thunder rattled with lightning and the rain came down all over our battery streets beating on the roofs of our huts. The heavens pounded down on this man's army in a ferocious violent manner. I remember thinking that God was still the Almighty and He was still in charge. He had the final control of the world in spite of the U. S. Army. I love storms to this day. The more lightning and noisier the storms are the better.

U. S. Army Signal Corps

My basic training came to an end the third week of November. We were again waiting for our new assignments. I had studied Radio Repair as a subject in high school. I spoke to the company commander asking for a possible transfer to the Signal Corps. Much to my surprise, I received special orders by the command of Colonel King to transfer to Fort Dix, New Jersey for further training in the Signal Corps. All my buddies in the 58th Battalion were on orders to go to Korea as had been rumored. I had avoided Korea for the time being.

I met three other GIs on the train from Fort Bliss who were also on orders to transfer to Fort Dix, New Jersey. The train from Texas was scheduled to arrive in Chicago the day before Thanksgiving where we would transfer to a train for New Jersey. However, when we reached Chicago, we decided that we would go home for Thanksgiving. One of us, Private James H. Scott, said he had a car and he volunteered to pick us up at our homes and we would all drive to New Jersey on Friday. The train we were to transfer to would not arrive in New Jersey until Friday anyway.

I took a cab to the airport and luckily, there was a plane getting ready to leave for Detroit. I bought my ticket and the clerk said, "I'll tell the pilot to wait for you but you'd better hurry." I was in uniform and it was amazing that everyone was happy to help a GI. I started for the plane, suitcase and duffle bag over my shoulder, when a redcap ran up to me and asked if he could help. "Yes!" I said, handing him my heavy duffle bag. Together we ran out of the building and on to the tarmac towards a plane waiting with the engines already running. They had the door of the plane open and a stairway up to the plane. As I ran, I reached into my pocket and grabbing a dollar, I handed it to the redcap as he gave me the duffle bag. I climbed the stairs where the airline stewardess showed me a seat in first class. "You're lucky soldier," she said. We don't often hold up a plane flight for just anybody and then let him sit in first class. Your lucky you're a GI." I knew I was lucky—I was in uniform.

My mother was surprised to see me home. It was a great Thanksgiving. All my relatives came over to see me. I had a great home cooked meal. I was happy to see my mother, sister and brother and sleep in my own bed again. Some of my friends and neighbors came over to see me and wish me luck in the army. It gave me a good feeling to see all of them. I was proud to be in uniform.

Friday afternoon, James Scott, my army buddy, with his car arrived as planned. We drove to Toledo and it was getting dark when a police car stopped us just before the Pennsylvania turnpike. Now what? I thought. Are we going to get arrested for going home for Thanksgiving? The officer's searched our car and we showed them our orders to transfer to

Fort Dix, New Jersey. They said, "Ok soldiers, you can go. But get that back license plate light fixed." I'll bet there was more to it then a burned out license plate light. I suppose they were wondering where these soldiers were going at this time of night.

Fort Dix, New Jersey

It was early in the morning when we arrived at Fort Dix. The MP at the gate directed us to a barracks where a sergeant took our papers and assigned us a bunk. It was Thanksgiving weekend and the sergeant was a little tipsy. He kept talking about the Second World War in Europe and how he had walked across Germany as a combat engineer: "I carried my coffin and a shovel all across France and Germany," he said. "I buried many of my buddies and I was ready for the same."

On Monday, I found myself in a new basic training company. I was starting basic training all over again. A week went by. Payday came, but I was not paid. I went to see the First Sergeant. He sent me to the Adjutant General—an officer who, I was told, was the serviceman's lawyer. I gave him my copy of my orders that I had received when I left Fort Bliss, Texas. He said that I would not have to take basic training again and he told me that the army would be sending all available men who had finished their basic training to Korea. "However, in your case," he said, "we are unable to find your papers. Until we find your papers, we can not do anything." Meanwhile, he put me on their casual list and excused me from taking basic training again. He gave me an advance on my pay and a pass if I wanted to go home for the Christmas holidays. I decided to hitch hike home over the Pennsylvania Turnpike and fly back after Christmas. I had no trouble getting rides.

For the next few weeks, I spent my time in the library and the PX. I wrote my mother that I would probably be sent to Korea. She wrote back that she was praying that I would not be sent overseas. Needless to say, I had missed another payday at the end of December, but this time—I didn't say a word. The second week in January, just as the adjutant general had told me, a notice went up on the bulletin board stating that all casual personnel would be put on orders to be transferred to Korea. Strange as it may seem, when the shipment of men went out, my name was not on that list. I surmised that my records had not yet been found. Once again I had avoided Korea. I preferred stateside duty if I could get it.

Fort Monmouth, New Jersey

Nine days after the New Year, my records were found and I was given orders for further training in the Signal Corps at Fort Monmouth, New Jersey. When I arrived at Fort Monmouth, I was told that although I had previous schooling in radio repair, unless I extended my enlistment to three years I did not qualify for radio repair school. I told them I didn't want to extend my enlistment to three years. My plans were to go to college with the GI bill after my eighteen-month enlistment. They said they would schedule me to study to be a Central Office Technician. This was a six-month duration. My job would be the installation and servicing of PBX telephone equipment.

I learned that I was the only short-term enlistee in the school. Everyone I spoke to was a long-term enlistee. I therefore made it my business to study hard. I was afraid that they would not let me finish. Six months later I finished at the top of my class. I received the United States Army Signal School Certificate as a Central Office Technician classification of 095.

I loved the school and even though we still had KP and Guard Duty, I was happy with this arrangement. I loved marching to school every morning in full "class A" uniform with a marching military band leading us.

The Signal School

Be it known that

PFC HENRY ARSENAULT

having been found qualified in the

CENTRAL OFFICE TECHNICIAN COURSE

at The Signal School
United States Army, is hereby awarded this

Certificate

In testimony whereof and by virtue of
authority vested in us by the War Department
we hereby affix our signatures and
the seal of this institution,

at Fort Monmouth, New Jersey, this 28th day of July 1942

ASSISTANT COMMANDANT

SECRETARY
Lt. Col., Sig. C.

COMMANDANT
Col., Sig. C.

V

Army Life

All the world's a stage
And one man is his time plays many parts.
William Shakespeare 1564-1616

"So you're Henry Arsenault!" the desk sergeant said, as I was being interviewed for final assignment after completing my school requirements. He looked up at me from his desk. "Your name kept coming up every month for the last six months. How did a 'short-timer' like you get into this school? If it wasn't for your straight 'A' grades, I would have had you out of here a long time ago."

He sent me for an interview to the Signal Corps Engineering Development Detachment on the Fort for possible job openings in the Signal Corps' Engineering Laboratories.

At SCEDD, a 1st lieutenant interviewed me. "I see by your records, you studied radio repair. What do you know the best?" he asked, "radio repair that you studied in high school, or central office that you just finished studying here?"

"Radio repair", I said, "I studied radio repair for two years in high school and I have a letter of recommendation signed by my school instructor listing all my studies."

"Hmm," he said reading the letter I handed him. Then looking down at the paper on his desk, he said, "We have an opening for a radio repairman in our Signal Corps' Coles Engineering Laboratory," he then looked me straight in the eye and said, "Do you think you can handle it?"

"Of course, that's the kind of work I was trying to get back at Fort Bliss, Texas."

"OK, it's your job!" he stood up and shook my hand. "Good luck, soldier."

I couldn't have planned it better. Life was great. It was a great job. I had the opportunity to work with civilian scientists as well as with German engineers who spoke with a heavy accent. They couldn't have been more polite and considerate. I was the only uniformed person in the Coles Short Range Radio laboratory section. I did miscellaneous tasks for them as needed, such as getting parts and hardware from the crib and testing short-range hardware and equipment for specific specifications.

I was promoted to a 'T5'. We use to say, "a T5 is a Corporal,—technician with brains." I received a permanent pass to leave the Fort. I had no KP or guard duty. I had a five-days-a-week job from 8am to 5pm, with weekends off with a permanent pass to leave the camp. What a life after basic training! Every month-end, after payday, we went to Manhattan where servicemen had free tickets to Broadway and radio shows and free lunches at the Soldiers and Sailors Club. We called it "the invasion of Manhattan Island." The fort had a good library, theatre and PX on the grounds with cut-rate costs that we could all afford. The PX served 3.2 beers to all soldiers for a small price. There were dances every Saturday at the PX attended by girls from and around the Fort. I didn't know how to dance and I was too shy to try, so I would just watch.

The GI Theatre Group

There was a theatrical group of GIs who were preparing to put on the play "Winterset." The Company Bulletin Board had a notice up asking for those who wanted to try out for this play. I tried out and was given the part of "Pedro, the organ grinder." I had a speaking part of two lines—"Whatsa da matter? You no lika the music?" It was a good play off Broadway in the thirties about gangsters in New York City. One poignant line I'll never forget is when the hero of the play states a chess move then asks a question. As I remember, he says, "White to play and mate in three moves. Why does white always win and black always lose? Suppose black were to win and white were to lose, what then? Well, then, black would be white and white would be black; as it often is; as we often are. Right makes white; losers turn black."

Every one in the play received a Commendation from thr Regiment Commander to go into our records. The theater group asked me to take the part of Groucho Marks in a play called "The Man Who Came to Dinner" but I would be leaving the Army before the play was scheduled to run so I had to turn it down.

In those days, everyone was proud to be in uniform. People gave us first class treatment wherever we went. At theaters, they always let us go to the head of the line. Everyone was friendly and spoke to us like they all knew us, as if we were relatives. I was getting the benefits and respect that was really earned by all the men and women who had gone over-seas and put their life on the line for the past four years for love of their country.

Manhattan's Broadway, Fifth Avenue, Time Square, was a land of magic that would be alive with people till all hours of the morning. It was similar to what Disneyland, Atlantic City, or Las Vegas is today. We visited the observation tower of the Empire State Building and we even went to Coney Island amusement park. Those month-end weekends in Manhattan were great. It was there where I tasted my first pizza pie, except in 1947 they called it "tomato pie."

Coles Laboratories

Another example I could cite to support the power of my mother's and my aunt's prayers that seemed to follow me, was during my assignment to Signal Corps' Coles Laboratories in New Jersey. One day, I was sent to help a captain and a sergeant move some crates of heavy radio equipment. A truckload of crates was to be moved to a warehouse for storage. "Climb on top of the boxes, Arsenault, and you can ride to the warehouse with us," the sergeant said.

The sergeant and the Captain were riding in the truck cab and I was sitting on top of the boxes on the bed of this stake truck when I felt the boxes I was sitting on move as the truck was rounding a curve. The next thing I knew, I was flying through the air with boxes falling all around me. I remember that it was the same feeling that I had experience in high school when doing flips in my cheerleading days. I had become quite good at tumbling. My trained reaction when being thrown from the truck was to tumble in a relaxed manner as soon as I touched ground. The truck screeched to a stop and the captain and the sergeant came running up to me as I lay on the ground.

"Don't move, soldier!" The sergeant shouted.

Why not? I thought, trying to feel my side where I rolled as I hit the ground.

At that moment the captain arrived at my side. Putting his hand on my shoulder, he said, "Don't try to move, not yet. How do you feel? Any pain anywhere?" He asked.

"No! I'm OK."

"Can you move your fingers?"

"Sure."

"Good, your neck's not broken. How about your toes?"

"Yes, I can move them too", I said, doing so.

"Good! Your back is not broken. Now wait, don't move not yet," the sergeant said as he lit up a cigarette and handed it to me.

I took a few puffs. "Can I get up now?"

"OK, but move very slowly and tell me if you feel any pain."

So I moved slowly and I could feel a sting along my upper right leg. "I'm okay", I said, "just some scratches on the side of my leg where my pants are torn."

"Soldier, there must be somebody praying for you," the captain said. "I thought we'd be picking up a bag of bones. You're lucky those boxes didn't fall on top of you. You sure you're okay?"

"Sure, I'm okay," I said as I stood.

"I want you to report to medical right away. Tell them what happened," he said. "It's in building A on the other side of those buildings across the field. Do you think you can walk that far?"

"Sure!"

"After you get out of there, take a shuttle back to the Fort and take the rest of the day off," the Captain said. "Tell them I said so. Let me know if there's any trouble."

"Yes sir," I said saluting him.

Letters

I reported to the medical first aid and the nurse put some medication on the scratches and bruises on my leg and sent me to the gate to catch a shuttle back to my barracks.

When I arrived there, I found a letter from my mother. "Are you all right?" she wrote, "Last night I had a dream that you fell off a truck. I could see you very clearly. You had a fresh haircut. I've been praying for you ever since."

Coincidence…who knows? I always thought my mother was a saint and had connections with God.

When I finished my eighteen months in the Army, I received the finest letter of recommendation I could have hoped for from R. A. Morris, Chief of Short-Range Equipment Section of the U. S. Army Signal Corps Engineering Laboratories. I thought I had been given a reputation that I will certainly try to live up to and hope to deserve.

HEADQUARTERS
SIGNAL CORPS ENGINEERING LABORATORIES
FORT MONMOUTH, NEW JERSEY

REFER TO:

ADDRESS REPLY TO:

22 March 1948

To Whom it May Concern:

This is to certify that the undersigned has known T-5 Henry Arsenault for 8 months.

Mr. Arsenault has a wealth of experience along radio technical lines and has served under me in the capacity of Technician 5th Grade, Radio Repairman for the past 8 months. The undersigned regards the abilities of Mr. Arsenault very highly and expresses the utmost confidence in him.

In my business dealings with Mr. Arsenault, I have found him to be sincere, reliable, conscientious, and tireless in his efforts to render service. He appears to be able to analyze any situation calmly and quickly under adverse conditions.

He is courteous, trustworthy, interested in his work, and loyal to his supervisors. He is cooperative in his work with others, is well liked, and respected by all his associates.

The services of Mr. Arsenault have been exceptionally satisfactory and the undersigned regrets that he will no longer be a part of this Office.

Very truly yours,

R. A. MORRIS
Chief, Short Range Equipment Section
Radio Communication Branch

They had been offered me a job as a civilian working in Coles Laboratories and after reading the letter, I wondered if I had made a mistake leaving New Jersey and this job offer.

The Dark Ages

These war years…remind me of what a college history professor once said: "We are living in the dark ages of mankind. A few thousand years from now, this era may well be looked on as barbaric and uncivilized. We are primitive savages, just barely out of the bush, mostly barbaric."

I believe that he was very close to the truth. If we consider the millions that died in World War II including the systematic execution of many millions in Nazi death camps, we can get some idea of what this historian was talking about. We have just begun our human existence and we have yet to become civilized. The human race has barely scratched the surface of enlightenment and man's humanity.

That's why I believe Christ came at the very earliest possible moment in time. He came at the very birth of a civilization that could grasp Divine understanding. Christ planted the beginning seeds of the dignity of man that could mature to a total humanized world in some future century.

Honorable Discharge

On March 31, 1948, my eighteen-month enlistment was up and I received an Honorable discharge from the Regular Army with the GI Bill locked in. Now I could go to college for eighteen months with all tuition, expenses plus 75 dollars monthly-authorized subsistence.

I was proud to have been a part of the Signal Corps Engineering Laboratories. President, Harry Truman, sent me a letter thanking me for serving my country. I'm sure all GIs who were discharged at that time received a letter from old HST, but I felt good getting my letter.

HENRY G. ARSENAULT

To you who answered the call of your country and served in its Armed Forces to bring about the total defeat of the enemy, I extend the heartfelt thanks of a grateful Nation. As one of the Nation's finest, you undertook the most severe task one can be called upon to perform. Because you demonstrated the fortitude, resourcefulness and calm judgment necessary to carry out that task, we now look to you for leadership and example in further exalting our country in peace.

Harry Truman

THE WHITE HOUSE

It took a year, after the fighting ceased, for Congress to officially declare the war over and the Victory Medal was issued to all personnel that were in the armed forces at the end of 1946, so I received mine just after my basic training. That's the only medal I received. That medal and my SCEL-DD letter of recommendation plus my letter from Harry Truman are my only trophies from my army days.

These army days taught me how to live harmoniously with many in one building. It also taught me that some hard work studying and with someone else's prayers could be a contributing factor for my successful enlistment tour in the United State's Regular Army.

VI

The GI Bill

The first twenty or twenty-five years of anyone's life are filled with education and training, both formal and informal. It's as if when you are born, you should be told, "Welcome to the human race. Now, here's what you will have to do and not do and here's what you have to know…" It's a catch-up game for the first twenty five years. After that, you spend the next twenty-five or thirty years trying to make the first twenty-five years of study and learning pay off.

From the beginning to the end of life, events such as world economic depressions, wars, marriage, children and death often change the direction of our lives and enrich or degrade us. Sometimes, these events destroy what we deem good in our lives. How can we explain this? How can we defend ourselves against a sea of trouble?

In 1950, President Harry S. Truman used his wartime powers to declare a 'police action' in Korea. This may have been a first on a world scale; Americans were now fighting in an undeclared war overseas. Many of my former high school classmates who had avoided the draft since graduation were now being called into service and sent to Korea. I knew that Korea was a hot spot back in 1946 when I first entered the army. All the officers were predicting that Korea would be our next war.

Luckily, I had already served my country and was out of the army by the time the Korean War started. My mother was still praying for me, I now surmise, and I once more was "delivered from evil." I consider war as evil. I didn't do a lot of praying in those days and that's why today I say, "someone was praying for me." And I'm sure that my mother and her two sisters in the convent were praying for me as they often told me.

I have come to believe that much of what happens tomorrow depends on what we do today. We are not designed by God to be contented cows, chewing on our cud. We all need to be challenged. We need challenges to experience the joy of success and the feeling of accomplishment. That's when fun comes into our lives.

With my honorable discharge on April 1, 1948, the GI Bill gave me a month of college tuition with expenses for every month of my enlistment plus 75 dollars a month subsistence. I first applied at the University of Detroit to enter its Engineering Department. Since I was pretty good at radio and telephone repair, I felt I should study and become an electrical engineer.

But, I did not have enough high school math and science. While I had studied radio repair for two years in high school, I had missed out on geometry, trigonometry, biology and chemistry. Since I would have to spend a year making up those subjects, I would only have six months of paid tuition from the GI Bill left to complete a four to five year endeavor. At that time, student loans, grants and scholarships were not prevalent.

Detroit College of Business

Following the path of least resistance, I decided on a Business School where I would earn an associates degree in two years without any make-up courses. This would be only three months short of what the GI Bill would pay. I would have to pay the last three months (a semester) myself. I had studied typing and business in high school. So, as in nature, I took the path of least resistance and registered at Detroit College of Business. And that's how I became an accountant.

Since all returning veterans were guaranteed their old jobs back, I returned to The Detroit News where I had been a part time copy boy for a year before I had enlisted and I was given an evening desk job in Display Advertising thus allowing me to go to college full-time during the day.

However, immature as I was, I kept that job for only two months. I wanted to spend all my time in school without work interfering with my studies. I know now that I would have been better off staying at the News where they were being so nice to me. It's another example of positive thinking: if you think you can—you can. And, if you think you can't, then you can't. If you begin with a negative attitude, you're two strikes down right from the start.

I now know that I could have worked, gone to school, and done even better, grade-wise, if I had thought I could and wanted it. At the Signal Corps School in the army, I had done just that. Also, six years later, I returned to Business College and did just that. I completed the last semester I had missed when the GI Bill had run out and I didn't have the money to finish at that time. This time I had decided I could, even though I was married with a family and I did.

I not only acquired the Associate's Degree, but I managed to get my Bachelor's Degree from the Detroit College of Business and my Master's Degree from the University of Detroit, thanks to the General Motors Employee Educational Reimbursement Program. So, I say, you have to believe that you can and you may surprise yourself as to what you really can do.

Education

I have often thought about our system of education. I feel and believe that every citizen in this great country should have the opportunity for as much education as they would aspire to have. The whole world should have free education for all who would pursue learning, without consideration as to race, color or creed. All world citizens, like the early Romans, should have the right to education at any school in the world any time in their life, with no tuition.

I believe as stated in the Declaration of Independence, that all men are "…endowed by their creator with certain inalienable rights; that among these are life, liberty, and the pursuit of happiness…" and I believe that "the pursuit of happiness" requires "education." I believe that this is a truth also "…to be self evident."

It is easy to observe that an educated person has the advantage over those who are less educated. It is obvious that life becomes better for that person and his or her world. Therefore, no one should be kept out of any university because of lack of money. The best thing that my service in the Army did for me was to give me the GI Bill. This Bill educated millions of Americans and gave us the chance to seek higher education. If you have the will and desire, your education should be free and unlimited.

Free college education should be the goal in this nation, the same as elementary education is today. Education should be a process that never ends. Trial and error is a method of self-education, but it is wasteful and time consuming. It is much easier to seek teachers who have spent their lives studying the subject and learn from them where the state of the art is today and start from there to make your contribution to this world.

The first few years into the fifties after I had left the army, I was completely concerned and absorbed with trying to get an education. There were certain habits I had to discontinue and certain new habits I had to pursue, such as reading and studying. The computer axiom, *garbage in, garbage out* is highly applicable here. Don't just read books—be selective. Read only good books, not garbage. It's bad enough that our environment fills our world with pollution and trash: the least we can do is to be selective when we have the option, and not fill our brains with pollution and trash. Don't just turn television on to see what's on; find out first from the schedule and then select what may be worthwhile, something that will make you a better person, not worse.

Christ said, "Seek and you shall find." I think that we should seek education and we will find it. Christ seems to be saying, "Don't give up." Psychiatrists tell us that we only use a very small part of our God-given brain. Every one of us has the capacity to do more and do better, if we try. Somebody said, "To try and fail is at least to learn; to fail to try is to suffer the immeasurable loss of what might have been."

During these early years of trying to obtain a formal education, I wrote a poem called *Relentless* to perk up my spirits.

RELENTLESS

The thought of the future;
Still inspires
Of castle and kingdoms,
And great empires.

A wondrous feeling;
For great achievement;
Though it be only
For self-appeasement.

My Blue Heaven

Where others have failed,
I will succeed.
Like a relentless tale;
I will proceed.

And though black seem the sky;
And failures in sight;
I'll never say 'die!'
I'll keep up the fight.

And when victory's at hand,
I'll say with a grin,
Shake hands with a man,
That knows how to win.

It was with these thoughts that I entered the fifties, full of hope and promise for the future. I had a good job as bookkeeper for Frank L. Mayhew, Wholesale Beef and Veal. I bought a new car and it seemed that nothing could go wrong. All I had to do was 'hang in there and fight'. I could hear in my mind's ear the words of, *Stout Hearted Men*, *I'll Buy That Dream* and *My Blue Heaven*.

VII

The Run Around

Every man's life is a fairy tale, written by God's fingers
Hans Christian Anderson

The year was 1951 when I met a girl named Margaret Elizabeth Foley. She lived only a few blocks from my house on Military street and we both had attended Holy Redeemer Catholic School. Although she was two years younger and an under-classman during my high school years, I had never met her. It wasn't until she was 21 and I was 23, that a mutual friend, Bernadette Mulligan, introduced her to me. Bernadette Mulligan was a member of a glee club of former classmates that I had joined after I was back from the US Army.

Bernadette was about five years older then I, and though we were friends, I noticed that when we went out together without the glee club, we would never go anywhere that her other friends might be. I guess she felt she was 'robbing the cradle' as the saying went in those days. One day, Bernadette said to me, "George, I've got the perfect girl for you, and I want you to meet her!"

Now, that's funny, I thought, why is she looking for the perfect girl for me? It must be the matchmaker instinct in older women.

"Is that right?" I answered. "I hope she's pretty."

"She's beautiful and she lives just four blocks from you."
"I'm game. When is this going to happen?"
"I'll ask her over tomorrow night and you be there to meet her."
"That's fine with me."

And that's how I met Marge. She was great from the beginning. She was as pretty as a picture and just as sweet as she was pretty. She was unpretentious, kind, easygoing, considerate and empathetic and wise. Everybody loved her. I couldn't help falling for her. She was so nice.

I grew up with the old song *I want a girl just like the girl that married dear old dad* ringing in my ears. And here she was. I had visions of someday marrying this perfect girl. I liked to picture myself as a perfect gentleman, a knight in shining armor on a white horse winning the heart of his fair lady with brave deeds. I use to tell everyone that my mother raised me to be a gentleman. The romance of my life would have to be a real lady, like my mother.

The age of chivalry is still here as far as I was concerned. I wanted (like in the song) *a Sunday kind of love…the kind to last past Saturday night…a little more than love at first sight.* She was my perfect girl. I treated her like a princess and she treated me like a prince. Who could ask for anything more?

After a few weeks, it seemed that I was seeing her every day. We just felt comfortable together and before long I was teasing her about marriage. "We might as well get married," I would say, "and stop all this foolishness of me coming over here every day. I could save on gas, and your parents insisting that you get home every night at a 'decent hour' is ridiculous. Your twenty one years old!"

"Not me!" she would answer. "I'm not the marrying kind!"

That was her standard answer, yet I continued with my standard question: "When are you going to say yes and marry me?"

One evening while we were out with another couple, the conversation turned to marriage and children. "Well," I said, "if I ever have any boys, they're going to learn the value of money early. I will expect them to have a paper route like I had and their own savings bank account to teach them the habit of saving, like my mother did for me."

"I think that if I ever have any girls," Marge said, "they will learn how to keep house and cook while they're still young and not like what happened at my mother's house."

"What happened at your house?" I asked.

"At our house there was my grandmother, my mother, my god mother and five children. We were never allowed in the kitchen between meals. We were never taught anything about cooking, cleaning or washing dishes. The three 'ladies' would do all that."

"They must have thought that three women cooking in the kitchen was already too many women," I said.

"I guess so, I'm not sure I could even boil water to this day."

"That's too bad," I said, "but you can read and anybody who can read can learn anything. There are *how-to books* on everything, especially cookbooks. Anyway, I'm on your side, Marge. I think that children should have chores and be expected to help around the house, and they should be included in all family affairs including the decision-making for family affairs. Children do not want to be a burden on their parents. I know I didn't and they do want to help and contribute. I know I did."

"Absolutely!" my friend Bob declared. "Children are part of the fun of being married and it's the family that makes it fun."

"Agreed," I said. "And here's another thing: I believe one should try to plan on having children while you're still young, say in your twenties. That way you're not an old man when they mature and you can still buddy-up with them for more fun...right?"

"Right!" Bob said, "like going fishing, camping, or to the ball game."

"That's the idea," I said, nodding my head in agreement.

The conversation turned to other things, but little did I realize what had just been discussed was giving Marge some ideas. Later that evening, when I was dropping Marge off at her home, I offered my usual query, "Will you marry me and stop all this 'I have to be home at a decent hour' business?"

She took me by surprise and said, "Maybe I will."

"What did you say?" I stammered.

"Maybe I will," she replied. "Tonight, when we were talking about marriage and children with Bob and Alice, I couldn't help thinking that 'your' children and 'my' children were 'our' children."

I couldn't believe my ears. Marge was actually saying 'maybe' after all these months of my teasing her. I wasn't prepared for that answer. I had anticipated her usual, "I'm not the marrying kind." This was a new answer. Now what do I do—I thought. I'd never gotten this far before.

"What do you mean by 'maybe'?" I asked.

"I have something to tell you," Marge said. Nine years ago, when I was thirteen, I had a brain tumor operation. I'm all right now, I guess, but before we can even plan on getting married, I want to have a complete physical examination at Ford's Hospital and get the doctor's okay."

"Are you serious? You had a brain tumor operation?"

"Yep!"

"But you're okay now…right?"

"Oh, sure, as far as I know. But I still want to be absolutely certain. So, that's why I said 'maybe' until I can get a doctor's clean bill of health I'm not marrying anyone. I was really sick nine years ago and it wouldn't be right to put you through the worry that my parents had at that time. I had double vision, loss of balance, nausea—-and terrible headaches.

My father and mother were worried sick, and my father, being a good Irish Catholic, got some water from Lourdes in France and blessed me with it every day. He also took me to see a very holy priest who was here at a Capuchin monastery on the eastside of Detroit. His name was Father Casey Solanus. Rumors were that he had performed many miracles and my father wasn't leaving a stone unturned. But I kept getting worse until finally I went into the hospital for more tests and then they operated. They operated right at the back of my head.

After the operation, the doctor told my parents that in about three weeks I could go back to school. Right after the operation, I felt fine. I didn't have those headaches or dizziness and no double vision. They called it a miracle," she said. "My parents had been praying for a miracle and the nuns in school told me that God must have great things planned for me. The nuns wanted me to join the convent and become a Sister of the Immaculate Heart of Mary…an IHM nun, like them, of course."

"Did you want to be a nun?"

"Not really. But when the sisters said I should, it caused me to think about it for a long time."

"Well, Father Solanus didn't say that you should become a nun, did he?"

"No, he just said that I would be all right."

"And he was right. You are all right now…. right?"

"Oh sure. But you can see why I need to be certain before I get married. It wouldn't be fair to you otherwise. That's why I always said, 'I'm not the marrying kind'. I always wondered if maybe I should have joined the IHMs and become a nun. "

"Well, as far as I'm concerned, you're fine by me….and that's what's important. Besides there's more than one-way to get to heaven…and being a good parent is a tougher job and more important than being a nun. Now, I'm not taking anything away from the nuns, but everyone has to look for their own vocation in this world. And I thing your vocation is with me."

Decisions

After leaving Marge, I was so confused that I didn't see her for three straight days. I was befuddled. I didn't know what was right and wrong. I asked my brother, Al, what he thought about my getting married. He looked at me with a puzzled expression on his face and said, "Well, if life gets dull, get married and it won't be dull any more." He was right. Life was never dull after my marriage.

I was unsure what direction would be the correct one for me to take. Maybe, I thought, the nuns were right and she should become a nun. Then, again, maybe I should be a priest. But where would the world be if everyone were to become nuns and priests? It would be the end of the world—no more children. No, I'm right! Everyone must find his own vocation in God's plan. The fact that she had a miracle and was 'saved for great things' as the nuns told her doesn't mean that she should become a nun. I'm happy with her and she's happy with me and that's what most important. I'm sure God didn't want the both of us to be miserable all our lives.

When Christ went to the wedding at Cana, I'm sure that he wasn't crying when he changed the water into wine and the people were rejoic-ing——celebrating for a good reason. Christ approved and sanctioned weddings, marriages, children, and families. I pondered and prayed for the right answer. To wed or not to wed, that was my question. I decided that she was the kind of a person for me and whatever children God might send us would be okay. I would be proud to say to my children, "this is your mother that I chose for you." And if the Almighty gives me fifty years with her or ten years or whatever, it would be better than no years. So, who cares what the doctors might say, I thought.

She can have her physical, but no matter what the results…. if she will have me as I am, then I will take her as she is. I'll insist that we be married even if the doctors give her a negative report. What do they know, anyway? I read where a doctor said, "half of what we learn in

medicine is wrong except we don't know which half." All her problems
are in the past anyway. What do I care about the past? It's now and the
future that is more important.

No one knows how many years they have left—even doctors. A brain
tumor operation when she was thirteen—humbug—I couldn't care
less. She apparently miraculously survived and that's it. So be it.
Remember, George, I said to myself, still reinforcing my decision, she
did finish high school and she was now gainfully employed with
General Motors as a teletype operator. You're not sick when you can do
that. What do you need, George? I asked myself. It's the writing on the
wall. Remember Father Solanus apparently did perform a miracle. She
may be a little unsteady in her balance when jumping over a puddle, but
she's just as normal as anyone else—and a lot smarter than your average
person and twice as nice—and she loves me. Who could ask for anything more? I wrote a poem for Marge. I called it *The Language of the
Heart*. I have lost the poem but the last stanza remains with me and
explains my feeling about love and marriage. It goes like this:

> *So, if my voice speaks not the words you seek.*
> *My actions are my words of smart.*
> *For words are not yet made to speak,*
> *The language of the heart.*

VIII

Still Learning

Life is a long lesson in humility.
Sir James M. Barrie 1860-1937

Bill Reeber was a very good friend of mine. His father owned a furniture store on West Warren and 23rd Street and we were in the Glee Club together where I had met Bernadette Mulligan. It was during this time when I was courting Margaret that my boss at GM Fleetwood plant sent me to a Dale Carnegie evening course at the GM Building on *How to Win Friends And Influence People*. Dale Carnegie had written a book by the same name

Public speaking was the main subject. But, I did learn something about how to win friends and influence people in taking this course that I have never forgotten.

The instructor said, "we can win friends by taking an interest in people. Talk about them and their plans, hopes, desires and their life. Take a sincere and honest interest and let them know it. As your homework, I want everyone to try this on a not-to-close friend or neighbor and make a report in a couple of weeks."

I decided that I would try this on Jim Reeber, Bill's younger brother. I would only see Jim when I would stop at their store. He never came with Bill and I when we would go out. Jim had his own friends; a few years younger then Bill and I. He had a girl friend that he was planning to marry. So, as part of my homework, every day I would see Jim, I would go out of my way to say hello and ask him about his upcoming wedding plans. He would go into detail of all the things that they were planning for before and after the wedding. Much to my amazement, Jim began to go out of his way to say hello to me. After a couple of weeks of this, Jim surprised me by asking me to be in his wedding. I had to accept but I sure was amazed.

Now, I'm not a person who aspired for a large family right from my youth. As I had often said, "a boy for you and a girl for me" seemed to me as the perfect size family for anyone. However, I had the occasion during the time I was courting Marge to be shocked with numbers in the size of a family. It happened one day when I was working repairing dealer radios in the basement of the Reeber Furniture Company.

"George," Bill said, "how would you like to go to a séance with me? I just delivered some furniture to this lady on 23rd Street and she told me that she holds séances. She said she'd give me a special free session. I said I'd let her know. I could call her and you and I can go over there and see what she has to say. How about it? I've never been to a séance and this might be interesting."

"I don't know, Bill…I personally don't believe in fortune telling. It's a lot of phony superstition, if you ask me. You can go, but leave me out. I think they're nothing but a con game to get your money. Harry Houdini and Sir Arthur Conan Doyle spent the last years of their lives exposing these frauds. They never did find a real spiritualist."

"Yea, I know, I know, but it's just for fun. I've never been to one and I'd like to see what they do."

"Look," I said, "I'm not paying for some fake telling me what I want to hear."

"Okay, don't worry," Bill, said, "it won't cost you a dime. I told you she said it was for free. I guess that was her way of tipping me for the delivering her furniture. It can't hurt anyone, and it won't cost you anything except time. What do you say, George? Let's give it a try."

"Well, okay, if you insist. But remember, I'm not paying her anything."

"We'll go tonight. I'll set it up," Bill said. "You'll see it'll be a lot of fun."

The Fortune Teller

It was a big two-family house with a flat upstairs and one downstairs. We pushed the downstairs bell, but it didn't seem to work. Then, we used a brass knocker shaped like the head of a bull with a large ring through its nose. Finally, a burly shirtless man opened the door. He was over six feet tall and, I'd guess, well over 200 pounds. He looked like he could be a wrestler and we could call him 'The Bone Crusher'.

"What do you want?" he demanded.

Bill and I looked at each other in amazement. I guess Bill hadn't seen this guy when he delivered the furniture. We were about to say "I think we have the wrong house," when a woman's voice came from inside.

"Who's there Waldo?"

Then before he could answer, the voice said, "It's all right, Waldo, it's the furniture delivery man and his friend. Let them in. I've been expecting them."

There wasn't much light in the house and from what I could see Mrs. 'Waldo' was a middle aged woman. Her hair was pinned up in a ball on top of her head, and she was wearing a purple robe. She looked like she was smiling behind her large gold-rimmed glasses. I 'think' she was smiling. It was either a smile or a sneer. It was hard to tell in the poor lighting.

"We came over for the séance, but we can come back some other time when you're not busy," Bill said as we both backed away.

"No, no, come right in," she said, coming to the door. "Waldo, get away from the door and let these nice boys in." The overgrown puppy dog stepped aside and Mrs. Waldo came out to usher us in.

"I've been waiting for you," she said. "Come right into my parlor." She led us into a small room to the left of the vestibule. It also was too dimly lit to see clearly. The room was empty except for about thirty folding chairs circling the wall and on a small table at the far side of the room holding a small lamp, which gave the only illumination. The blinds on the only window were pulled down.

This must be were Mrs. Waldo holds her séances, I thought. What, no crystal ball?

"Take a seat," she said very pleasantly, pointing to the folding chairs. "Take any one of them, please."

We certainly had our choice. Bill and I took two seats together at the opposite end of the room. "Is this all right?" Bill asked.

"That's just fine," she said as she closed the door to the room. "Now, don't be frightened. I'm just going to turn off the light. I cannot communicate with the spirits of the other world and foretell the future with the lights on. I must also have complete silence, or the spirits will leave me." With this, she touched a switch near the door where she was sitting and the room instantly turned pitch black. We were in total darkness. Usually you can see light around the cracks of the door to an outside room, but the vestibule we had come from was itself so poorly lit that nothing came through the cracks in the door. It's a good thing she said don't be afraid, I thought. I wondered what was next on her agenda.

Then we heard a load moan and a screech and some weird noises and garbled talking that didn't make any sense. She must be trying to call the spirits, I thought. Why did I ever let Bill talk me into this mess anyway? I'll be glad when we're out of here!

Speak to me, O spirits," she finally uttered in some understandable tones. "Tell me the future of these two gentlemen." He voice had changed to a deep guttural sound. "Tell me the secrets and let me look far into the future, O spirits of the outer world. Yes, yes, Bill will prosper and marry a beautiful girl. He will have many children."

Then the tone of her voice seemed to change again and after more indistinguishable sounds and garbled words sounding like a foreign language, she said, "George will marry a beautiful girl and he will prosper and have a house full of children. Both Bill and George will have many blessings." More garbled words that we could not understand. Suddenly she gave a loud screech and shouting "No!" she turned on the light and muttered in her own voice, "I cannot foretell anymore...the spirits have left me...you must go!"

I looked at Bill and stared at the spiritualist. Her head bowed, she seemed upset with her hands over her ears. Suddenly, she sprang to her feet, and opening the door, she said, "You will have to excuse me, gentlemen. Please go. I am tired now. Perhaps some other time I can tell you more of your future." With this, she stepped out into the vestibule and opening the outside door for us, she said, "Go, and read chapter 6, the 20th to the 27th verse of St. Luke in the Holy Bible." With this, she stepped out into the vestibule and opening the outside door for us, she said, "Go! Read chapter 6, the 20th to the 27th verse of St. Luke in the Holy Bible."

Now, that's a switch, I thought. I'm expecting witches and devils and she tells me to read the Bible. Maybe she's a religious nut. The burly Mr. Waldo was nowhere in sight. We were only too glad to get out of there. What a strange and eerie experience. I wonder what made her stop so abruptly?

"What a weird place, and what a nut that dame is," I said as Bill and I entered the car. You don't think that she saw something that she didn't want to talk about? Do you?

"She sure had me wrong, "Bill said. Many kids—ha! What a laugh."

"What about me? Imagine me having a house full of kids. Now, that's a bigger laugh. I wonder what Marge will say when I tell her that she's going to have a house full of kids."

"Well, this one was free, and that's about all it was worth. I wonder why she stopped so suddenly, Bill mused. "Almost as if she saw something bad that she didn't want to tell us about."

"And, what about the Bible chapter 5 of St. Mathew," I said. "I wonder what that was all about."

"Maybe it says to pay her for her séance. Either that, or she's starting her own church. All you need to start a church these days is the Bible."

"I've heard that sometimes spiritualists mix religion into their séances," I added.

"It sure was different than what I expected," Bill said. "The hollering and screeching, I expected. But I also expected to see some floating horns and ghostly faces. I guess she's not into that yet."

"She really didn't tell us much of anything," I said. "But what do you expect for nothing anyway?"

Blessed Are They

That night when I got home I looked up the 5th chapter of St. Mathew and it turned out to be the Sermon on the Mount. It didn't have any special meaning to me. The next day when I told Marge about this spiritual episode, we both had a good laugh. "Imagine me," Marge said, "having a house full of kids. I like children, but how many is a house full?"

"It depends on how big the house is, I guess," Shaking my head. "Two children—a girl for you and a boy for me. That's my idea of a perfect family. Two is more than enough for anybody."

With that we quickly forgot the whole incident.

IX

Love And Marriage

When a man and woman are married
Their romance ceases and their history commences.
Abbe de Rochebrune 1740-1810

I gave her a diamond engagement ring for Christmas. We planned our wedding for September. We were waiting until September, because I had purchased a new Ford two door in June of 1951 with a year's payments. I would finish my payments on the loan in June of 1952. This gave us a couple months to save some money for our wedding.

On September 6, 1952, we were married at the Holy Redeemer Church. It was a pretty big wedding. Bill was my best man and my brother was an usher. I think that was a mistake. I now am an advocate for family, your brother, as the best man. But when my brother got married a year earlier, he had his best friend as the best man. So be it. We had a nice brunch at the Botsford Inn and we had our honeymoon at Niagara Falls. It was a nice week and the beginning of a new life.

My Blue Heaven

We had rented a two-bedroom upper flat at 1707 Livernois in Detroit. Like the song *'Tea For Two'* we were in our blue heaven. But Marge wanted children and I thought, okay,—here we go. We had talked about children when the priest was giving us the premarital instruction. I remember that Father Peter J. Forbes, pastor of our church telling us, "God's primary purpose of marriage is to bring children into the world. That's why God made man and woman and unites them in the Holy Sacrament of Marriage."

We knew what the Catholic Church taught about the many blessings of a family and we were in agreement about the fun of having a family with children. And it was the idea of our having children that had caused Marge to change her mind and say 'yes'. So there were no surprises. But guess what? After six months of trying, Marge was not pregnant. Now, we were finding that having children was not that easy. Marge asked our doctor.

Why, doctor, can't I become pregnant?

"I'm afraid that you will probably never have any children," he said. "It's your biological makeup. You will probably never be able to conceive. But if it's any consolation to you, there are many people like you. You could adopt a child if you feel you need children."

I was not for adoption. I thought that if God figured that we should not have children, then, that decision was good enough for me. Not having children is another honorable vocation. We could just take more vacations and travel and have fun. Children are expensive and they take up a lot of your time. Not to mention the anxiety and grief that children sometimes give you. No children—that's okay with me, and I think that Marge would go along with this.

But, a month after the doctor's prognosis, Marge became pregnant. It was hard to believe. Another miracle? But with Marge, you never knew what she could do. It reminded me of something I read about old Henry Ford the First having once said, "The difficult, we do immediately; the impossible takes a little longer." I'm told that the Seabees and the Army Engineers also used Ford's statement as their motto. Where Ford got it is a mystery to me.

Baby and Me

Nine months later, the first-born. Mary Ann, named after my mother, was born feet first. "Lucky you came to Ford Hospital for this birth," the nurse said to me when she showed me the baby.

"Ford Hospital is accustomed to these types of births and we're all set up for them. The baby was given a clean bill of health."

Two days later, the doctor told us that the baby was not doing well. Because she was not able to take nourishment from her breast feedings, they thought that there might be an obstruction in her throat. But, the X-rays proved negative. The decision was made to put her on formula and stop the breast feedings. Finally, we were told that all was well again; the baby was doing great on formula and gaining weight.

Taking care of the first baby is not easy for new parents. Baby Mary Ann was just a few months old when she ran a fever. Marge called the doctor. "You must come over to the apartment; our baby has a fever of 101.

"Just bring her to the office," he said.

"Doctor, it's winter and I'm not taking her out in this cold weather. You must come here," Marge said with the righteous determination of a mother protecting her child.

"But Mrs. Arsenault, we do it all the time. The cool air will help bring down her temperature. But if you insist, I'll stop over on my way home."

"I insist!" Marge said.

The doctor made a house call. He left the motor running in his Cadillac with the door wide open as he raced up to our second floor apartment with his little black bag. He gave the baby a shot and went running back down the stairs to his car. It was evident that he was not worried about the health of our baby. Running after him I asked, "How much do I owe you?"

"Twenty dollars."

Hurriedly I pulled a twenty out of my wallet and handed it him. "Will she be all right?"

"Oh sure. If she's not better tomorrow, call me he said as he climbed into his Cadillac."

Baby Mary Ann was better the next day and the second crisis for the new parents was over. The words of a song echoed in my head, *Just Margie and me and baby make three, we're happy in my blue heaven.*

New House

About a year later, Marge was expecting a second baby. When we told the landlady the good news she said, "You know that an apartment is no place to raise children. I'm sorry to tell you, but you will have to move. I'll give you two months to find another place."

So there we were; expecting our second baby and we get our eviction notice. Having read about the houses being built for veterans with the GI Bill for only five hundred dollars down. This was another benefit I received for my service time. We began to look at new houses for GI Veterans. We looked in the city of Livonia and in Allen Park. Because Allen Park was closer to Detroit, where I worked and where my widowed mother lived as well as Marge's parents, we finally bought a new house in a builder's development project in Allen Park. But our house would not be ready for some six to eight months so our second baby, Patrick Joseph, was born on June 23rd of 1955. I knew our landlady would not kick us out, but, I also knew she was right about raising children in cramped quarters not being a good idea. She very kindly said that we could stay until our new house was built which would be sometime in the fall.

Allen Park

We moved to our new Allen Park home where it seemed each year or two the patter of little feet continued until we had a large family of seven children. That's a lot of names to come up with for each baby. What's in a name? All the children's names had various rationales behind them:

The first-born was named Mary Ann after her grandmother Arsenault. Also, the year of 1954 was called the Marian Year by the Catholic Church as a year dedicated to Mary the Mother of Christ. So, it seemed to be appropriate for the year.

The second born in 1955 was Patrick Joseph and named after Marge's brother who was earning his way through the University of Michigan Law School as a cab driver. Also, my father's first name was Joseph.

The third born in 1956 we named Margaret Elizabeth to please Marge's godmother Margaret Elizabeth who was seriously ill at the time. The fourth born in 1958 was named Robert Ernest in memory of my brother who had died so young and my father, who was called Ernest, his second name. The fifth born in 1959 was Mark Anthony in honor of Marge's two favorite saints, St. Mark and St. Anthony.

The sixth born in 1960 was Aileen Therese in honor of Marge's sister Aileen who had died at the age of twenty-one from leukemia a dozen years before. Marge really loved her older sister dearly and had watched her waste away from this dreadful disease. Whenever Marge would speak of her, she always had tears in her eyes.

In eight years we had seven children. But, who's counting and all I know is that Marge wanted a big family and she was happiest and healthiest when she was with her children. I had a good job with GM and we could take care of all of them.

"After your miraculous cure at age thirteen," I would tease her, "the nuns at school told you that you were destined for great things. Well, if they could see you now! You with a house full of kids would surprise them."

"My children are my great things," she would tell me. "My blessings are my children."

"Well," I would answer in jest, "if we have enough of them, maybe one will turn out all right."—Silently praying they all would.

Marge loved her family. She was happiest when she was with them. She had the patience of a saint and the understanding and unselfish love that only a good mother could have. She was quick to praise and slow to find fault. Even her corrections were more of discussion of right and wrong with her children than decrees. She was a teacher and a mother. When she talked to her children, she would also listen to them. The ability to listen that was the key. She treated each one as an individual with his or her own personality. She never tried to dominate them. I was happy to have Marge as the mother of my children.

X

Events

Events of all sorts creep and fly exactly as God pleases
William Cowper 1731-1800

In the summer of 1961, Marge began experiencing terrible headaches and earaches. She was beginning to have trouble remembering telephone numbers, even her mother's number. She would go to tears as she struggled to remember.

As weeks went by, her headaches and earaches gradually increased in frequency and severity. Her balance was becoming more impaired and there were indications that not only her memory was diminishing but also her ability to reason and carry on a conversation. Her logic was becoming more and more confused. She would loose track of what day it was, or even what time of the day it was. And when I corrected her on this, she would see her error and go into tears because of her mistakes. She wondered what was happening to her. Her vision began to play tricks on her and sometimes she would see double. All this was happening during the summer of 1961.

At first when the headaches occurred, I thought it was just the normal headache that everyone sometimes gets. I tried not to think about what might be the real reason. The explanation was far more complex than a simple headache and the remedy perhaps far more serious. Still, I grasped at every straw to avoid the conclusion that lingered with me as the only plausible explanation. The symptoms all pointed to a repeat of the symptoms of twenty years ago that indicated a brain tumor. I was hoping that if I ignored what might be reality, maybe it would go away. I remembered somebody saying, "People who are cured by a miracle, never die from what they were cured of." I quickly accepted this—hoping it was true.

I remember the first time I became aware of how severe her headaches were. It was about two o'clock in the morning when she woke me up. "George, you have to go out and get me some aspirins. We're all out and I can't stand this headache."

"What?" I asked, looking at the clock, "at two in the morning, you want me to go out and buy aspirin? Are you kidding? Is the headache that bad?"

"Really bad…and I'm not kidding!" she cried. "You have to go!"

"Of course I'll go." I said as I got out of bed putting my pants on over my pajamas.

Pulling out of my driveway I thought—here it is two in the morning—where am I going to find a drugstore open at this time of the night? I didn't realize how many aspirins she must have been taking to run out like this. I spotted a bar and thought that maybe they would have aspirin. But they had closed at 2 a.m. Then I spotted a restaurant that was open. I went inside and they had little packages of aspirin. I raced home to find Marge waiting at the door.

The next day we went to see our family doctor. After his careful examination, he recommended that we see a neurologist or neurosurgeon. I knew where he was leading us. We made an appointment with Doctor Aaron, who was the protégé of the neurosurgeon Marge had twenty years ago. Her original surgeon had died and Dr. Aaron took over the same office.

By this time, Marge's condition had worsened. Each day seemed to bring new symptoms. She was now dragging her left foot and needed assistance to walk. The doctor gave Marge a careful examination and as I had feared, he diagnosed Marge's trouble as a possible recurrence of her brain tumor. "I'll have to find the original records of the operation of 1942 to see what the prognosis was after the operation," he said.

"Do you think this could get any worse, Doctor?" I asked, hoping for some encouragement.

"One never knows in these cases, but it will be well for us to restudy the original case and go on from there."

"But why…" I asked. "After twenty years?"

"We don't know. There's much we don't know about the brain. We don't know why a thirteen year old has a brain tumor nor a man at the age of fifty who was in good health has one. What medicine knows about the brain can be put in one book. All we know after some very unpleasant tests is that the tumor is there and that alone. Our only treatment at this time is to attempt to remove the tumor by operating and/or using radiation to shrink the tumor."

"Isn't there any other possible explanation for her symptoms?" I asked.

"Yes, but we'll be able to know more after we see the prognosis notes of the original operation."

"When will that be?"

"This week," he said. "I'll call you."

A week later, Dr. Aaron's nurse called to tell us the doctor had found the records of the original operation and would like to see us.

"Well doctor, what did you find out?" I anxiously asked the doctor while Marge was waiting in the examination room. "Contrary to your belief," the doctor said, "no tumor was removed in the 1942 operation"

"But doctor," I said, "she got better and everyone was under the impression that the operation was a success."

"It was a success, because all the symptoms had disappeared. But you can see here in his notes written immediately after the operation, the doctor states after he opened the area at the back of the head, "…and observed *tissues of insignificance*. I remember Marge telling me that she had had radiation treatments after the operation for any remaining tumor.

"The tumor may still be there," he said. "The radiation treatments were used to shrink the tumor. It is quite apparent that the operation did relieve the pressure in the head and radiation may well have shrunk the tumor. This would account for the remarkable recovery that she did have, but," he continued, pointing to the papers on his desk—"these notes of the doctor clearly indicate that they did not see any tumor. Probably because of the tumor's location being more in the center of the head and it would have been too dangerous to go any deeper. Therefore, after observing 'tissues of insignificance' the procedure was just to close the incision. Her remarkable recovery was otherwise unexplainable. She is a very remarkable girl," he said. "It's her will and determination that has served her well all these years."

"Do you think that this is the same tumor?" I asked.

"I don't know," he said. "I think that we should admit her to the hospital where we can take some tests and then we will be able to tell what it is and what can be done for her. We'll have to play it by ear."

Harper Hospital

Two days later, Marge was admitted into Harper Hospital for tests. I knew that these were serious procedures because every time they did a test, I had to sign a paper to approve the procedure. And these tests always involved the operating room. I found out that in one test, they shaved a spot on the top of her head and drilled a hole to remove fluid and then X-rayed and replaced fluid. Other tests involved inserting dyes and more X-rays. Every day, Marge had another test and every day there was another paper for me to sign.

Testing

Weeks went by and Marge's health in the hospital became progressively worse. I was sure that the tests were taking their toll. You take any healthy person and submit them to the same tests and they wouldn't be feeling too well either. After the first few tests, Marge was unable to get out of bed by herself. She had a wheelchair along side her bed to go to the bathroom and to go to the next test. The only two things that she could do were to smoke and watch TV. She watched all the soap operas every day. It helped to take her mind off her own problems.

One afternoon, when I arrived at the hospital from work, I found Marge in bed with the foot of the bed elevated about three feet higher than the head. "What's going on here," I asked the nurse in charge.

"Marge had a test today that caused her blood pressure to change and the doctor ordered this position for eight hours to prevent her from having severe headaches. We'll be around shortly to lower the foot of the bed."

"How do you feel, Marge?" I asked.

"I'm okay I guess. But will you please light me a cigarette. They won't let me smoke unless someone is with me."

"Is that right?" I said, lighting two cigarettes at a time as in the movies. "Why did they do that?"

"Well, earlier today after one of the tests, I tried to light up and I dropped the match. The bed sheets caught fire and I yelled as I tried to pat the fire out. The result was just a little burn hole. But now I can't smoke alone."

"Did you get any burns?"

"No, just scared. My balance and coordination aren't what they use to be."

"I know. I'm glad it wasn't any worse than that. Maybe it is better that you don't smoke unless someone is here to help you.

"Did the doctor come in to see you today?" I asked.

"He never fails."

"What did he say? Anything new?"

"Not really. He just said that he would be talking to you as soon as all the tests are completed."

"I'll give him a call tomorrow."

Operation

The next morning, when I called him on the phone, the doctor told me that they needed another test before he could make any diagnosis. That night after work when I went to the hospital, I found Marge resting comfortably, but none the better.

Another week went by and the tests were completed and the results were in. The X-ray specialists had made their report. The labs had all finalized their reports and the time was here for the doctor's analysis and decision for the course of action. I did not really want to hear it when the doctor called me aside at the hospital and said, "There are no indications of a brain tumor in the original area at the base of the head. However, this time our tests indicate that there is a tumor in the frontal right lobe area."

"Does this mean another operation?"

"I'm afraid we have no alternative," he said. "Her condition is deteriorating and the best way to handle this is to operate immediately and remove the tumor. This time we will be able to see the tumor and the prognosis is good. Also, she is young and that is in her favor. We can hope for a complete recovery if the tumor is not malignant. She has a good chance that it is not malignant based on her history of the prior tumor."

"What are our chances, doctor?" I forced myself to ask.

"Very good for this condition. I'd say fifty-fifty."

That didn't sound very good to me—fifty-fifty. I passed the word at home to the children and told them to pray for their mother. I also called St. Mary Magdalene School and asked the principal, Sister Janet, and the good nuns to remember Marge in their prayers. I sent a telegram to Father Methodius (Dick Telnack) with whom I had graduated from Holy Redeemer High School and who now was a Trappist monk at Our Lady of the Holy Spirit Monastery in Conyers, Georgia. I figured that he had a direct line to the Lord. The telegram read:

> Father Methodius
> Marge scheduled for a brain-tumor operation.
> Doctors give her a fifty-fifty chance.
> Need prayers! George Arsenault

Dick Telnack was the smartest guy in my high school class. In 1946, when we graduated, we were in line to be drafted into the army. So, as I had stated earlier, Dick enlisted in the Marines for two years and I enlisted in the Army for eighteen months. After he got out of the Marines, he joined the Trappist monks, fed up with the way the world was going, I guessed, he took the bull by the horns and joined the Trappist. He's only a little guy, but to me, he's a giant among men. I had already written to him about Marge and I felt that he could help with his prayers. I thought to myself, when all else fails—try prayer. It's strange how we ask God to understand our plans and us yet and we give little thought to understanding God and His plans.

Is there really power in prayer? I asked myself. It's times like this that we want to believe. Didn't Christ say, "If you have the faith of a mustard seed, you can move mountains." and "If you ask the Father for anything in my name, He will give it to you. Ask and you shall receive. Seek and you shall find. Knock and it shall be opened unto you." These were the words I needed to keep telling myself.

Success

The operation was scheduled for eight in the morning of Halloween, the day before All Saints Day. If we ever needed all saints, it was today, I thought as I drove to the hospital at about 6am. It was the old army game, hurry up and wait. After the surgery, the doctor appeared in the doorway of the waiting room and motioned for me to come out in the hallway.

"How is Marge?" I anxiously asked.

"She's fine," he said. "We were able to remove about ninety percent of the tumor. It was the size of an orange. We just kept taking off a little at a time until bit by bit we had most of it. We kept her semi-conscious in order for her to help us identify the area we were working on. It is amazing that with this size tumor, she was able to function as well as she had. Also amazing was when she was taken to the recovery room she asked for a glass of water and she surprised us all when she took the glass and lifting it directly to her mouth, she drank from it. She couldn't do that before the operation, you know. It's almost miraculous"

"When will I be able to see her?"

"In about an hour they'll be returning her to her room. You can see her then."

She was lying in bed with her head completely bandaged. She was looking up at me and smiling, "Hi honey."

"Hi," I said. "How are you feeling?"

"Okay, I guess," she said. "I've got a little headache and I feel weak, but outside of that I'm okay."

"The doctor said you were great during the operation and the operation was a success. You'll be coming home in a few days," I said wiping a tear from the corner of my eye.

"The operation wasn't so bad," she said. "It was easier than delivering a baby."

"Well, the worst is over and as Shakespeare said, '*all's well that ends well…*' *and Amen.*"

The next day, when I arrived at the hospital after work at about suppertime, I did not find Marge in her room. I went to the nurse's station. "Where is my wife, Margaret Arsenault? She's not in her room. Did something go wrong?"

"No, Mr. Arsenault, nothing went wrong," a nurse said. "I think that you will find her having a cigarette in the visitor's lounge."

"You have to be kidding," I said. "That's a lot of trouble for you people to wheel her down to the visitor's lounge just to have a cigarette."

When I arrived there, I found Marge sitting up in a chair just as pretty as a picture and smoking her cigarette. She smiled when she saw me and said, "Hi honey, are you surprised?"

"Surprised?" I stuttered. "I'm amazed. Where is the nurse? And where is your wheelchair?"

"The nurse is around somewhere and I didn't need a wheelchair. I walked here with the nurse. I wanted to surprise you," she said.

"Surprise me? You astounded me," I said. "I must be dreaming. I can't believe it. Two days ago you couldn't go anywhere without a wheelchair. Today, you're walking. Here we go again…another miracle. You amaze me."

She walked back to her room, arm in arm, with me. She hadn't walked in six weeks. Our prayers were answered, I thought. The doctor said she would go home in a few days and he was right.

I found out that prayers were said by all the parish school children every day for the past six weeks that she had been in the hospital. The principal, Sister Janet asked for prayers every day over the loudspeaker. Sister Janet's and the Mother Superior, Sister Frances' requests for prayers by the Saint Mary Magdalene Parochial school children and the prayers of Father Methodius plus all of our family had paid off. All of my five oldest children and the school had been praying every day for Marge's recovery.

Marge was coming home. This was another of her miracles. She was a fighter from the word go. She now could be with her children who were not allowed to visit her in the hospital for over a month.

Janet Frances

Was Marge all right after this second brain tumor operation at the age of thirty-two? Outside of the fact that she had to grow a new head of hair, she was better than all right. In fact, a year later in 1962, we were waiting for the birth of a new baby. The baby would be a cesarean birth, as the doctors had advised for her last three babies. The doctor had picked November 9 as the delivery date. But that was the day my dad had died and my mother suggested that the baby be born on a different day. So, the doctor said, "No problem, we'll just make it November 8."

So, on November 8, Marge delivered a beautiful new little baby girl. We named her Janet Frances for the two nuns that had prayed for Marge's recovery.

XI

Adversity

The flower that follows the sun does so even on cloudy days.
—Robert Leighton 1611-1684.

With all our past troubles, the world went on its own way unmindful of my own problems. The year is 1963. In June, Pope John XXIII died. In August, the 'hot line' between Washington and Moscow began operation. September 21, President John Kennedy announced that he was sending Defense Secretary Robert McNamara and the Chairman of the Joint Chiefs of Staff, General Maxwell Taylor, to South Vietnam to review our military effort.

October 1 was a beautiful fall day in Michigan. I was on my way home from work—only a few blocks from home—when, hearing a siren blaring, I pulled my car to the side of the road as an ambulance sped by me with its lights flashing.

The way he's driving and the direction he's going, I thought, he must be headed for Outer Drive Hospital with someone in deep trouble.

Years ago—at Holy Redeemer Catholic School—the nuns told us, "whenever you hear a siren, say a prayer for somebody in trouble." I guess there are some things from out of our past that we never forget.

I was turning the corner of our street, when I spotted a group of neighbors in front of our house. I pulled over to the curb. As I got out of my car, I heard someone say, "There's the father."

Oh—oh…what's happening here? I hesitatingly thought and thinking to myself, do they mean me? I'm the father they want?

John, my next-door neighbor came up to me. "George, there's been an accident. The ambulance just left with Marge. You must have just passed it. Go to Outer Drive Hospital—hurry!"

A uniformed police officer came over. "Your wife has been burned. Your neighbors are looking after your children. So, I think you had better go direct to the Emergency Room at the Outer Drive Hospital."

I hadn't even noticed the police car across the street. Now its flashing red lights added to my apprehension of misfortune.

A cold sweat popped out on my forehead. "Are my children all right?"

"The children are fine." John said pointing towards our house. "Ira (his wife) is with them. You'd better get to the hospital right away. Don't worry about the children—we'll take care of them until you get back. Just go!"

Outer Drive Hospital

At the hospital, I found Marge in the hallway of the Emergency Room sitting upright on a chair. She had a white sheet wrapped around her shoulders. She was fully conscious.

Seeing me, she said in a whisper, "Don't touch me. I'm burned from my neck down to my waist."

"What happened Marge?" I asked with tears in my eyes.

"This is probably the dumbest thing I've ever done," she said. "I was cooking supper and I had on my new blouse and sweater you just bought me from Hudson's. When I turned, I must have been too close to the gas stove and the next thing I knew, my blouse and sweater were on fire. I ran outside screaming for help when Ira, next door, heard me and came running over. By the time she got there, my blouse and sweater already had burned itself out. Some of the neighbors put this sheet around me and somebody brought me a chair to sit on."

"You must be in terrible pain," I said. "Have they given you anything for pain?"

"Yes, they gave me a shot of something. I only feel pain in my arms and neck and some pain on my chest."

"Why are you sitting in a chair? Shouldn't you be lying down?" But then, I thought, how could she lie down with those burns?

"They don't want me to lie down. They said my back was the most seriously burned and that lying down would make it even worse."

"Were you able to sign in and give them the information they needed?"

"Yes, I had to."

"Have they called Dr. Leonard (our family doctor)?"

"Yes. He's on his way with a burn specialist now."

"I think I saw the ambulance you came in. It passed me on my way home from work."

"They had to call two ambulances. The first ambulance did not have a seat for me to sit on and I couldn't lie down. So, they called a van type ambulance where I could sit on a wheelchair."

"The doctors are here now." A nurse approached. "We'll be taking your wife up to her room now, Mr. Arsenault. If you will step over to the desk, they will complete the papers and tell you her room number."

"Keep a stiff upper lip, Marge," I said trying to encourage her. "I love you, Marge and I'll see you in a few minutes." I turned and quickly walked to the emergency desk.

Third Degree

As I pushed open the door to Marge's room, I heard the burn specialist and our doctor talking to her.

"Can you feel anything?" the specialist asked as he placed his two fingers on the raw skin of her back.

"No," Marge said.

"How about this, how does this feel?" the doctor asked, as he touched all around her back.

"No," Marge answered.

"Can you feel this?" as he touched her arms and neck.

"Yes, that hurts," Marge, said.

"Does it hurt only when I touch it?"

"No, it hurts the same."

"I'm going to be frank with you, Marge," the specialist said. "You're badly burned and it will take a long time to heal. But you were lucky that you didn't get burned on your face and that your hair didn't catch fire."

The doctor motioned me toward the door. "Marge, I'll be just outside," I said as I walked to the door.

"I'll be right back."

In the hall, the doctor said, "Your wife has a forty percent burn area. Much of it is third degree burn and that will require skin grafting. Our biggest problem now will be to avoid infection."

"But…why isn't she in more pain…and complaining more?" I asked.

"Part of it is the shock effect to the nerve system. And remember we have her under medication to control pain and shock. Also, when you have third-degree burns, you've destroyed all the nerve cells in the area and there is no pain when the nerve cells are dead. If you feel pain, it will heal. If you don't feel pain, it will not heal by itself."

"How much are third degree burns?" I persisted.

"We know it's her entire back. We don't know how deep. We'll just have to wait and see. What will not heal will be third-degree burns. But our first worry is infection. If we can beat that and get most of the burns healed, then we can think about skin grafts. Infection is always the enemy because a third-degree burn is an open wound that does not heal."

Recuperation

It was now apparent that Marge would be hospitalized for many months. My mother took our 1 year old, Janet and our 3 year old, Aileen. I hired a nanny to watch over the other five children when they came home from school and to see that they were fed. I wanted the children to have good meals and I would 'catch as catch can.' Daily, I would go to work at 7:30 am. After work, I would stop at the hospital for a few minutes to check on Marge. Then, I would go home to check on the rest of the family. Mark, the 5 year old, was in kindergarten. Robert, who was 6, was in first grade. Margaret, 8 year old, was in third grade. Patrick, 9 years old, was in the forth grade and ten year old Mary Ann was in the Fifth grade. Many days, I would get a baby sitter in the evenings and go to the hospital. The days of October were filled with these maneuvers.

In November, the specialist brought in a therapist trained in bathing burn patients. The therapist explained that it would take weeks of careful bathing of Marge's burns to help her fight infection and heal what was healable.

"She will sit in a special chair and we will lower her in a specially medicated tub of warm water," he said. "Daily baths will speed up the healing process and help fight against any infection."

The baths started. Every day they lowered Marge into a tub of warm water. Marge told me that the water would turn red by the time they raised her out of it.

"I bet that really hurts," I said.

"Worse then anything I've ever had!" she said. "Sometimes, I think I'd rather jump out of that window. But then I think of you and the children…and I would never do that."

"No, don't you ever do that."

"Oh, I know, I know. I won't. I think of you and the children and that helps. And I pray a lot. That helps. I wish I knew the Stations of the Cross for this rosary."

"Maybe I should talk to the doctor about these baths."

"No, don't," Marge, said. "They're all very kind and gentle. They're just doing everything that they can for me. But now that you mention it, please pick up a carton of Viceroys for the therapist. I know that's what he smokes. He's been so nice to me."

Healing

November 22nd, the TV and the radio are all talking about the assassination of President John F. Kennedy in Texas. As I drove routinely from work to the hospital, all the stations on the radio were saying the same: "Our 47 year old President, John F. Kennedy, was fatally shot while riding in a motorcade through Dallas, Texas today."

"Marge," I said as I turned on the television in her room. "The President has been shot."

"Yes, I know. Turn that damn TV off! Spare me the details," she snapped.

"The bath pain must have really been bad today," I said as I turned off the TV.

"It was…and the water is still turning red. I've got enough trouble now and I don't have the patience to listen to someone else's agony."

"I know it's painful, but the baths must be working. You've avoided infection—and see: a lot of your burns have already healed."

"Oh sure. But it still hurts like hell—every damn day."

"Well, don't give up," I said. "Keep up the fight. We'll get out of this thing yet. I promise."

"That's easy for you to say, you don't have to bear the pain. But don't worry. I've gone this far. I can go the rest of the way."

"Good for you," I said. "Everyone's praying for you. The kids…all of St. Mary Magdalene Grade School are saying a prayer for you every day."

Because most of the burn areas were left uncovered and loose gauze just barely covered the rest, I could see that at least half the burns were healing. But her back still looked raw. As the doctors had said, most of her back had third degree burns. Skin grafting operation is next, I thought.

I was right. On December the first, the doctors told us of their plans.

"We would like to schedule a skin graft operation for the last day of the year." "Marge, we will attempt to graft skin from your legs to all the third degree area of your back in this one operation. If we're successful, you can start the new year right." He looked from Marge to me. "We want Marge to quit smoking as soon as possible so as to clear the blood stream of constricting nicotine. This will enhance the body's ability to successfully take the grafting and healing process. That way we can hope for less grafting needed at a later date if any at all."

"We can do that…right Marge?" I said.

"What do you mean…'We'? "

"I'll quit with you, Marge. Everyone should quit anyway."

"Well, I guess I can quit if I have to."

"Sure you can. We can do it together."

"By the way Doc, will Marge be able to come home for a couple days for Christmas?" I said.

"We'll see if we can arrange a furlough for her."

XII

Smoking

Man is, properly speaking, based upon hope; he has no other posses-
sion but hope; this world of his is emphatically the place of hope.
—Alexander Carlyle 1748-1825

I bought every book I could find on how to quit smoking. The Surgeon General of the United States had just that year declared that smoking can cause cancer, so there were a lot of books out on the subject. I recall *'How to Quit Smoking Or Double Your Money Back'* and *'Smoking Is For Suckers'*. Another was a medical review with graphic pictures of lungs and vivid stories about the slow strangulation of emphysema, heart trouble and mouth and throat cancer. Ugh! I just skimmed though that one. It wasn't going to be easy for two people like Marge and me who each smoked a pack or more a day, to quit cold. But all the books suggested cold turkey was the best way. Even though we both smoked like chimneys, Marge and I agreed that we should go cold turkey. In addition to saving money, we would both improve our health, and Marge's upcoming skin grafts would have a better chance for success.

December 8th was the date we chose for cold turkey. I bought 2 one-dollar cigars the night before my farewell to smoking. My mouth was like a furnace as I smoked one cigar after another. I had a burnt taste in my mouth. That'll teach me, I thought. I discovered that the first twenty-four hours are the worst. It takes that long to get the nicotine out of your blood stream. And, it takes about two weeks to get it out of your other systems. I believe I read that it takes five years to clear out your lungs alone. The book experts had suggested substituting another habit to take the place of smoking. I chose salted pumpkin seeds. Marge chose gum. Whenever we had the urge for a cigarette——which was all the time——we would be chewing gum, or eating pumpkin seeds instead of smoking.

When I awoke on the morning of the eighth; I had been off cigarettes for eight hours. But all day I kept reaching my shirt pocket for a cigarette. As the book had suggested, I didn't tell anyone that we had quit smoking. I thought to myself smugly, look at them, acting like nothing is wrong. They don't even know that I haven't had a cigarette all day. People offered me cigarettes and didn't even ask questions when I said "no thanks."

"Well, Marge, did you stop smoking?" was the first question I asked when I got to her room.

"I've done pretty good," she said. "I only had two cigarettes all day."

"What's good about that? I've had none, zero, cold-turkey remember our agreement?"

"Oh, I remember. But it's not easy."

"Yes, I know it's not easy. But it'll get easier the longer you stay away from them," I said as I tried to persuade and encourage her. "That's what the books say. It's really a matter of memory. When you first quit, you remember every minute that you're not smoking and you are aware every minute that you're not smoking. You will watch others light up and find yourself reaching for a cigarette. But as time goes by, there are minutes that you forget that you're not smoking. And I guess these minutes will lapse into hours as days go by. After a few weeks, these hours of forgetting that you're not smoking will lengthen into days. When that happens, we've got it licked. We'll finally have that smoke monkey off our backs. Alleluia. If it's not cold turkey, it's just a prolonged agony so I'm told.

"OK, OK, cold-turkey. If you can do it, I guess I can too."

"I know you can and I know that it's hard to quit. Remember my quitting for twenty-four hours the first day of Lent every year for Lenten penance? That was agony. I can remember waiting for the clock to hit midnight at the end of that day. Remember how I would have a match lit and the cigarette in my mouth waiting for that first puff? What a slave I was to tobacco. So I knew the first day would be bad. But today is a tiny bit easier."

Christmas

Marge came home two days before Christmas. The house was filled with Christmas cheer. The children were elated. Although she could not wear any dresses and still had these loose bandages around her, we had two happy days with Marge home again and running her household. She still could not lie on her back and had to sleep on her side. But after three long months without her children (the hospitals did not allow children to visit), Marge was back home for a few days with her children. The children happily waited on her and Mary Ann, our ten year old, was at her beck and call.

On December the 30th, grafting took place on her back. Two strips of about one inch wide and eight inches long were taken from the upper thigh of each leg and placed across Marge's back. When I saw her after the operation, not only her torso but both upper legs were bandaged.

"How do you feel?" I asked her when they finally let me in the room.

"Good!" she said. "When they put me out, all the pain went away. It was the first time in three months that finally I was able to get some rest."

"Well, at least that's a plus."

"Did you talk with the doctors?" she asked.

"Yes. They said the operation went very well. They think that with a little luck this one operation may be all you will need. Now, that's really good news."

"One operation is all I want," Marge said. "But what I really want is my walking papers so I can get out of here and go home."

I remember the radio singing, "I Love you because", "I Want To Be Around", and Tony Bennett was singing "The Good Life". Even Richard Chamberlain, TV's Dr. Kildare was singing "All I Have To Do Is Dream". On this last day of 1963 we were looking forward to 1964 as a better year for all of us.

Routine

As the weeks went by, I developed a routine. I would see the kids off to school in the morning before going to work. I would work till four and go right to the hospital from work to see Marge. During the weekdays I had hired a nanny to feed them and tidy up the house. I also had a local teenager to baby-sit and look after the kids from time to time. My widowed mother took baby Janet to live at her house. On weekends, my mother and the baby would stay at our house. I didn't eat at home except for a late bite. I lost fifteen pounds during these months of running to the hospital. I would normally get back home about six thirty or seven in the evening. I had discovered another way to loss weight—have a tragedy.

Winning

The last week in January, I was with Marge in the hospital during her suppertime at about five o'clock. This had been my usual routine these past four months. Marge was sitting in a chair. The bandages had finally been removed and I could see for the first time the tops of her legs where the skin graft had been taken—both legs they were blood red. I was amazed that they would remove the bandage so soon. I surmised that the doctors must want the air to get to them to help the healing.

"Marge…your legs…look how red they are! They must hurt like hell. They look like they're inflamed. I wonder if they took the bandages off too soon?"

"They're almost all healed," Marge said. "The doctors said that the redness would eventually fade away."

"They don't look healed to me…"

"Well, they are. Go ahead and touch them. You'll see."

I touched the top of her legs. They felt just as smooth as a baby's skin. "I'm amazed," I said. "I'm glad that they're doing well. I was told that they just take only the top layer of skin——like tissue paper——and that they graft it to the burned area and it grows new skin. It's like plant-ing seeds. Pretty neat."

"I guess that's the way it works. They're pretty smart."

"I was told that the doctors gave you a good report this morning. All the skin graft is taking—is this true?"

"I guess it is. They put me on special medication to help prevent infection."

"Well, I sure hope that it does the trick."

"Me too. Did you ask them when I'm getting out of here? My back is better and I don't have bandages any more."

"They tell me that it'll be after they're sure that you will not get any infections on the wounds. They have to keep a close eye on you——but I'm sure it will be soon. I think we're winning!

Her back was getting better. The nurses were applying cocoa butter and that made it feel better. Marge just loved it when the nurses spread cocoa butter over her back each day.

On January 15, 1964, the doctors declare Marge's skin graft operation a huge success. "Marge will not require any more skin graft surgery," the doctor said. Alleluia!

Home Again

The second week in February, Marge was given her long awaited walking papers and officially discharged from Outer Drive Hospital after five long months. I was able to hire a housekeeper to help Marge for five days a week. Marge was home but she could not do very much. It was difficult for her to walk and she still needed help to get her strength back. We had a full house. In our three-bedroom ranch home, I had built two rooms in the basement (our lower level) with a bathroom for the three boys. The two oldest girls were in one bedroom, the two youngest were in the other and Marge and I were in another. The weeks went by and Marge seemed to be getting stronger.

Relapse

It was the seventeenth of March—St. Patrick's Day—when I heard a thud. I had just gone down the basement to check on the boys. Marge had just finished saying good-bye to the housekeeper for the day and had gone to the bedroom to lie down. I raced up the stairs looking for Marge. As I entered the bedroom, I saw her lying next to the bed, a small cut on her forehead.

She was unconscious. She must have passed out and hit her head on the bed as she fell to the floor, I thought. Quick, I said to myself, call the doctor at his office. Maybe he's still in.

"Put a cold cloth on her forehead and stay with her," the doctor said over the phone. "If she doesn't come to in ten or fifteen minutes, have an ambulance take her to Outer Drive Hospital. Have them call me from there."

I had put Marge in the bed and I sat there talking to her. "Marge, wake up. Are you OK? Please wake up, Marge." I kept looking at my watch. After fifteen minutes, I called the ambulance.

XIII

Trouble

When troubles comes from God, then naught behooves like patience;
but for troubles wrought of me, patience is hard—I tell you it is hard.
—Jean Ingelow 1820-97.

At Outer Drive hospital, Marge was still unconscious. "Will she be all right, doctor?" I asked.

"I think so," he said. "We've given her a shot and now we'll have to wait until she comes around. After she's awake for a while, you may be able to take her back home."

Two hours later and Marge was still out. Our family doctor had arrived. He had a worried look on his face when he came over to talk to me. "I'm admitting Marge into the hospital."

"Why isn't she waking up, Doc?"

"I don't know. But I suspect that these past few months have been very hard on her and her old problems may be coming back. You know that she blacked out in the hospital two weeks before we released her."

"No, I didn't know that."

"You better go home to your children. You can't help Marge here," he said. "She's in good hands now. Call me in the morning."

"Thanks Doc. I guess you're right."

"Don't worry," he said. "She'll be better in the morning."

That night I called my mother and brought her to our house to look after the children for the weekend.

Next morning I raced to the hospital. Marge was better. At least she was conscious. "Hi Marge, how's it going?"

"Hi," she said. "I'm feeling weak. I don't know what happened to me."

"I found you unconscious on the floor in the bedroom. I was really worried about you when you wouldn't wake up. But you're in good hands now. The staff remembers you from the burns. They really like you and I know that they'll take good care of you."

"I don't remember a thing until I woke up here. I guess I fainted at home and you brought me here. Do I have to get new walking-papers to go home again?"

"We'll ask the doctor as soon as I see him. He's around here somewhere." Just as I said that, the doctor came into the room.

"Well, our patient is a little better than when she got here last night. Will you excuse us Marge, while I talk to your husband," he said as he motioned me into the hall.

As soon as we were in the hall, he said, "We're going to keep her for a few days. We're treating her for a high fever. I don't know what is causing the fever and I don't want her to catch pneumonia. We're giving her antibiotics."

"She says she's very weak," I said.

"I'm going to call her neurosurgeon, Dr. Aaron, for his opinion. This problem may be related to his area of expertise. She needs rest so don't stay too long. I'll talk to you tomorrow after I have spoken to Dr. Aaron."

The next day Marge seemed better. At least her voice seemed a little stronger. I saw the doctor at the nurses' station.

"Hi Doc," I said. "Did you talk to Doctor Aaron?"

"Yes, and he concurred with my diagnosis. So we decided that it would be better if Marge is transferred to Harper Hospital where Dr. Aaron will take over her care."

"The next morning, I was at the hospital when the ambulance came to transfer Marge to Harper Hospital.

"You're going for a ride today," I said to Marge as they wheeled her down the hall to the ambulance.

"I can use a ride," she said. "This time, maybe I can see some sights."

I followed the ambulance out of the parking lot. When, they turned on their siren and flashing lights, I knew I would never be able to keep up with them, so I didn't even try. By the time I arrived at Harper Hospital, parked the car and found her room, the nurses had already given Marge an alcohol rubdown.

Marge was getting first class treatment. I was glad. I knew that no matter where Marge went, Marge would capture the hearts of all around her as long as she could talk. She just had a way with people and knew how to talk to them. I think that it was the way she would empathize with them. Everyone loved her. After visiting with her, I felt that she was already better then she had been at Outer Drive Hospital. The drive had done her some good.

I went home to check on the children then returned to the hospital around Marge's suppertime. As I walked from the parking lot, I passed a young street vendor who was selling bunches of red roses out of his old beat-up-car in front of the hospital.

"Buy your best girl some roses," he said. "Only five dollars."

"Not today, but save me a dozen later for my best girl."

"I sure will," he said. "Maybe tomorrow?"

"Maybe."

Coincidence, I thought. Then I remembered: in route to the hospital I had heard on my car radio, "*I want some red roses for a blue lady*' so, I turned to the vendor. "On second thought, give me a dozen roses for my best girl right now." And I handed him a five-dollar bill.

"Now you're talking," he said as he handed me a bouquet of red roses. Dr. Aaron was in the hall outside of Marge's room.

"How's my best girl, Doc?" I asked.

"She's very thin and very weak," he said. "We'll have to try to put some weight on her and build up her strength."

"She likes malted milks," I said. "I've been giving her malted milks every day at home for the past month and she really likes them."

"Fine," he said. "Anything that will put weight on her will be fine. We will be putting her on a special diet for that."

So everyday, I brought Marge a special malted milk that I made at home. I had bought a real malt mixer and I was even putting an egg in it. After a week, she seemed to be getting a little stronger and she was even walking a little.

After another week, it was April. Marge was still very weak. I was on my way to her room when I heard someone call "Mr. Arsenault, Mr. Arsenault." Looking around, I saw a nurse waving at me to come over to the nurses' station.

"You're Margaret Arsenault's husband?"

"Yes."

"Your wife is very ill. She has a Staph pneumonia with a high fever. We have given her medication and she is sleeping now. Please try not to disturb her and don't stay too long. Also, Dr. Aaron wants you to call him at his office tomorrow morning."

The next day, the doctor told me over the phone that Marge had Staph pneumonia and they'd had to transfer her to a private room because that type of pneumonia is very infectious.

When I saw Marge later that day, she was really down. I realized that she was in an isolation ward. I had to wear special white robes and a mask to go into her room. "The doctor's say you have Staph pneumonia and they want to do a tracheotomy to help clear your lungs." Marge started to cry. I said, "Marge, it will be all right, they said it will help you."

Well, they had really done it this time. They had taken her room-mate and kind nurses away from her and now, anyone she saw would be wearing a mask. She had always enjoyed having someone to talk to in her room. I think that Marge knew more then I did about what a tracheotomy was and the consequences. Dumb as I was, I should have realized that when they wanted me to sign for it, it must have been serious. I should have asked more questions. I should have stalled more before I signed that paper. Her neurosurgeon had said that it was to make it easier for the lung therapist and not his idea.

The next day, I found Marge in an oxygen tent. She opened her eyes and seemed to smile. She couldn't say anything. I discovered that with a tracheotomy, you couldn't talk because they put a hole in your throat for you to breath through. And when they use the suction hose to clear the fluid from your lungs, they have to go through that hole. Now, they've even managed to take her voice away from her, I thought.

That night, I got a call from my mother. "George," she said. "Baby Janet is very sick. We took her to the doctor and he put her in Providence hospital. He said she has Staph pneumonia."

My brother had taken my mother and the baby to the doctor because of a high fever. I called a baby-sitter, and then headed for Providence Hospital in Detroit. It was a thirty-minute drive from Allen Park.

Providence Hospital was on West Grand Boulevard, about fifteen minutes from Harper Hospital. I found baby Janet in a room by herself. She too was in an oxygen tent. She had an intravenous needle in her foot. That's strange, I thought. They were giving her something through the foot. I've never seen that before. Out in the hall, I found the doctor. "How my baby Janet?" I asked.

"You have a very sick baby, Mr. Arsenault," he said. "She has Staph pneumonia and to make matters worse, she's very anemic, which probably explains why she became infected. But, we got her just in time, I think. Tell me, is she a bottle baby?"

"Yes, I think she is," I said. "She loves her bottle."

"Well, it's time to take her bottle away from her. Any fourteen month old baby should have been on solid food long ago."

"Janet has been staying at my mother's house," I told him. "My wife, Margaret, is also in the hospital, at Harper's. She has Staph pneumonia and is in an oxygen tent and she has other complications." I went on to explain Marge's problems and he said, "You certainly have your hands full."

I sure do, I thought. As if one isn't enough, now I have to worry about two. It may have been my fault. I had probably carried that Staph germ inadvertently to Janet in her weakened anemic condition. Maybe in those plastic malted milk containers that I carted back and forth every day from Harper Hospital for Marge's milk shakes.

XIV

Two Hospitals

With the fearful strain that is on me night and day,
if I did not laugh, I should die. Abe Lincoln—1809-65

Every day from then on, I would first go to see Janet. I left work at four o'clock and got to Providence around five. I would stay about fifteen or twenty minutes then go to Harper hospital, another ten miles, to see Marge. Marge wasn't getting any stronger. She seemed to be sleeping most of the time. I would have to wake her up each day when I got there. "Marge!" She opened her eyes and seeing me, she would smile.

"Marge, baby Janet is in Providence hospital and she too has Staph pneumonia and is in an oxygen tent."

Marge looked away.

"I want both of you to get out of these oxygen tents," I said.

Marge closed her eyes. I'm not sure she even heard what I said. She still had that hole in her neck and she couldn't talk to me so it was a one-way street.

Janet Frances

Two weeks went by and low and behold, they both were out of the oxygen tents. Janet was eating from a plate and drinking from a glass. What a change! I would help feed Janet with a spoon. She even had regular food, like fish and chicken. She was doing very well and when I visited her each day, she would smile and laugh. But, when I left the room, she would cry. So I started to play a little game with her. I would go out the door, and she would start crying and I would pop back in and say boo. She would stop crying and laugh. I would do this several times and when she was laughing I would leave to go to Harper hospital to see her mother.

Janet was discharged from the hospital the last week in April. She went back to my mother's house with new feeding instructions. Marge, still unable to walk, was still being feed intravenously. I prayed that Marge too would soon be discharged. I prayed that in May, she would come home. Every day, on my way to the hospital, I would say the rosary as fast as I could so I would say as many as possible in that short time. I stopped off at St Patrick's Church near the hospital to light a candle and pray for Marge. The church was mostly empty and I would have to hide my face on my way out with my handkerchief to hide the tears streaming down my face. I sure felt sorry for myself.

Red Roses

On May 26th, I sat with her, not speaking, I was just glad to be there with her in the event she would wake up. At the end of my daily visit, I bent over her and said, "Marge, keep up the fight!"

She opened her eyes and tried to speak. I had learned that if I put my finger over the silver washer in her throat, she could utter some sounds. So I put my finger on the hole and with my ear near her, I was able to discern her saying in a low raspy voice, "keep up the fight when you're hardest hit."

My mind flashed back to an old anonymous poem that we both had known—*Keep up the fight when you're hardest hit; it's when things seem worst that you mustn't quit.* She was trying to tell me that she was hardest hit and things were worse. She closed her eyes and fell back to sleep.

The following day, her eyes remained closed. All this sleeping was probably medication. I wondered if it was necessary.

The next day, the 28th of May, I got a call from Dr. Aaron at my accounting office.

"Mr. Arsenault, you had better come to the hospital right away."

"What's wrong, Doc. Is Marge worse?"

"Yes, I'm afraid so."

"You mean I should leave right now?"

"Right now! You'd better hurry. I'm afraid we're going to lose her."

"I'll be right there!"

I called my mother and her parents and told them what the doctor had said and I left for the hospital as fast as I could.

When I arrived at Marge's room. She wasn't there. They must have moved her again, I thought. I discovered that they had transferred her to the Maternity section. Very appropriate, I thought. She should feel at home there after giving birth to seven children. I'll bet this was the only place that had a vacant room and they didn't want her to die in the section where all the nurses knew and loved her so well.

Marge was in an oxygen tent with all kinds of tubes and machines around her. I reached into the tent for her hand. It was cold. But I could still see her breathing though her eyes were closed. I then went out into the hall. Marge's parents and her brother, Patrick, and her sister, Mary, were in the waiting room down the hall. We paced the floor for about two hours quietly. Finally I said, "Why are we all waiting here?" No one answered me. I knew why we were all waiting and they knew too. We were waiting for Marge to die, but no one had the heart to say it. I certainly would never say it.

"Then why don't you all go home," I finally said. "I'll let you know if anything happens." I felt that they were relieved.

"Be sure and call us immediately if anything happens, or if you need something."

"Of course," I said.

Then they all left. I didn't think that they all would leave. I was alone but I felt better. I was alone with my own agony. I went into Marge's room. She seemed to be having difficulty breathing and her hand was turning bluish. I pushed the aid button. The nurse came in immediately, took one look and said, "Oh my god, I'll get the doctor," and left the room.

I knew what the nurse meant. This was the event we all had been waiting for and now was the time Marge would leave us. I decided to leave too. I went to the elevator across the hall and down to the main floor. I went outside, hoping to get some fresh air and clear my head.

I saw the flower vendor, still there, standing near the curb.

"Red roses for your best girl," he said.

"Not this time," I said with tears in my eyes. "I think I'm going to lose my best girl—she dying."

I turned and raced up the hospital steps, the vendor follow me. Taking my arm, he said, "No, you won't lose her. I'll go with you and we'll pray to God. I'll give her this bunch of roses. They're for life and health. Come on, lead me to her room and we'll pray to Jesus Christ together."

The elevator was waiting when we got to it. I pushed the button for the seventh floor. When the elevator door opened on her floor, I saw the doctor and the nurse in the hall outside Marge's room.

I knew by the look on their faces that Marge was gone.

"I'm sorry," the doctor said. "Your wife has just died. Do you want to go in and see her?"

"Oh my god, we're too late," I heard the flower vendor say.

"You mean," I said, "Marge is gone…She's not here…Gone. She's really gone," I said with tears running done my face.

"Yes, she's gone," the doctor said sadly. "Do you want to see her?"

"You say she's gone and you want to know if I want to see her. No—I already saw her with all those tubes and machines around her. No! I don't want to see her if she's gone. Just leave me alone."

XV

The Philosopher

The idea of philosophy is truth; the idea of religion is life.
—Peter Bayne 1830-96

When I went into the funeral parlor to see Marge for the first time since the hospital, I didn't know what to expect. I had told my brother Al, to take care of all the arrangements, and my mother took care of the children. When I saw Marge lay out in her casket, she took my breath away. She was so beautiful. She looked as beautiful as the first day I had met her. She looked as if she were sleeping like the sleeping beauty in the fairy story. I felt that I could go up to her and kiss her and she would wake up. They had made her look like the photographs my brother had given them. She had been so thin and pale and now she was back looking like the girl I had married twelve years ago. But, when I touched her, it was like touching a piece of wood. I knew that she wasn't there.

After the funeral, Marge's mother, Lily, said, "Marge will be able to take a lot better care of her family now that she's in heaven. She would never leave her family and not take care them. She'll watch over all of you."

Just nodding my head, I thought to myself, small chance of that ever being true. I did not mean that Marge wouldn't help her husband and family if she could and God knows she's a saint if anybody is, but, like that old Baptist's hymn, *That Old Rugged Cross*, life can sure get rugged. Like that other old Baptist's song, I would rather be *Leaning on the Lord, Safe and Secure.*

I wrote a letter to my cousin in Montreal about six weeks after Marge died where I said, "I don't know what my job is anymore. To pay the bills, I can manage. To be a mother to my children seems almost impossible. To find someone who could take their mother's place seems improbable if not impossible. The woman would have to be "tops" and these are few and far between. What are not already married are in a convent. No! I'm afraid, it will never happen. Just tell some woman, "I want you to meet a widower who has seven children." And that woman will turn and run and I wouldn't blame them. Because it's summer time, I am able to hire teenage girls to baby sit during the day for five dollars while I work. Come September, these teenagers will be back in school and I will have to hire someone, perhaps to stay all week and be off on weekends. I'll try and get someone for forty dollars a week with room and board."

I found myself living each day with invisible tears in my eyes, incredible pain in my heart, and indelible memories of what I had and lost. Not a fast lost but a long, hard, painful lost. I find myself feeling sorry for myself and for the children because they now have no mother. "She'll watch over all of you," her mother said. Oh, sure! How?

Depending on Marge now that she is gone or any Saint for help doesn't seem to fit. It's hard to understand what concern or power any saint would have for our intercession with God. Furthermore, most of our prayers are directed to God. Saints are secondary. Why bother with saints if you can talk directly to the boss? Why a middleman? Especially when the boss is so omnipotent, benevolent and understanding. I'm not saying that saints are not made and that they don't have a special place with God. This may be, but I think that the title is a degree of honor mostly. Who knows what influence they have after death?

The few saints that the Catholic Church has proclaimed are not even the tip of the iceberg. There must be millions and millions of saints in heaven if you define saints as being associated with God. Yet many pray to saints and I don't think there's anything wrong with that. God knows us and understands us better then we understand Him. So, he gets the message anyway.

Luckily, God chooses to understand us even if we don't understand Him. So, I believe there are millions of saints who the Church have never proclaimed and who never had a religious vocation in the Church.

My idea of a saint is a person who lives by the Golden Rule and does his duty to his fellow man and keeps the philosophy of the Ten Commandments in his everyday life. It's a person who can do his job to the best of his ability and then some. A person does his best and a little extra. It's that little bit extra, unselfish effort for others that gain saint-hood in the eyes of God, I think.

That's why mothers are mostly saints. Can you think of anyone who has more unselfish love then a mother for her child? And they are con-sistent...always faithful and true. As Caesar said, "I am as constant as the Northern Star."

Christ was more than a saint, but he didn't spend all his time in the temple praying. No, he was out among the people of all walks of life, helping them, loving them, and teaching them to love one another.

Trying to understand death after a traumatic loss leads one to reli-gion and God. Hungry for the right words, I turned to books. What did the great thinkers of our world have to say about death? Augustine, Aquinas and Luther were too academic for my needs. Descartes was interesting with his "*I think, therefore I am*" thesis. And Nietzsche left me cold with his *superman*. Plato came the closest to the truth that I was seeking. And Christ and the Bible, I suspect, is the truth.

Searching the Bible and reading the Dialogues of Plato, I did find some consolation. Both Christ and Socrates had a lot to say about death and they both faced an untimely death. Each had time to think about their inevitable demise.

Christ said, "Father, if it be your will, remove this cup." Christ knew that after Good Friday, there would be His Easter Sunday with all of its glory. Yet given his choice as a human, he would rather have stayed with his job of teaching and helping people and avoid this death on the cross. But God has some plans that are not easily understood by humans and take priority to our will. So, "Thy will be done." Christ said.

As the Son of God, Christ knew that this was the best way. *Anyone who does the will of my Father will never die. And, though he is dead, he will live.* Strange words the assertion that God knows what he's doing, began to make some sense to me. I have to admit that if God is omnipotent, then He must be a lot smarter than I am. So be it. It behooves me to go along with Him, even when I don't understand what He's doing.

Then sometimes, I think that when things go wrong, it's not really God's will in the true sense of the word. God has willed that there be a certain cause and effect in nature. If we jump off a bridge, well, we just have to suffer the consequences. God is not likely to perform a miracle to save some dummy that won't use his head. God gave us brains, He expects us to use them. And if we're going to be stupid about it, then cause and effect is still God's law.

Socrates said, "Life is a journey from the mortal towards the divine." Socrates believed that a philosopher spends his life preparing for death. He said, "we should keep ourselves pure until the hour when God himself is pleased to release us from this life." This statement eliminates suicide and genocide as a solution to our problems. Socrates said that the oracle [God] that had directed him throughout all his life did not oppose this last judgment of death the citizens of Athens had given him.

So, therefore, the end result must be good. *And those of us who think that death is an evil are in error.* It was as if Socrates was reading the 23rd Psalm *though I shall walk through the valley of death, I shall not fear,* when Socrates said,...*know of a certainty, that no evil can happen to a good man, either in life or after death.* His dialogue anticipates the Christian philosophy when he states, *we ought not to retaliate or render evil for evil to anyone.* Christians use the *Golden Rule.*

It is interesting to note that Socrates did not fear death. "The fear of death," he said, "is indeed the pretense of knowledge and not real wisdom. No one knows that this death they fear as the greatest evil may be but the greatest good. A man who is good for anything," Socrates stated, "ought not to calculate the chance of living or dying; he ought only to consider whether in doing anything, he is doing right or wrong, acting the part of a good man or a bad man."

Socrates further said, "the unexamined life is not worth living...the difficulty my friend, is not to avoid death, but to avoid unrighteousness; for that runs faster then death."

Billy Graham, the evangelist, was quoted as saying when speaking of death,...if we live with God, we will live until God calls us and we die, and then we will live forever with God.

It appears that the best argument for religion and God is death. If there is a life after death, then it behooves us to live in such a way as to warranty a good eternity after death. Life is short and eternity is a long, a very long time.

The riddle of life: Why are we here? Where are we going? And what will we do when we get there? The meditation on these questions leads one to theology for a logical explanation. I was compelled to acknowledge an existence of some supreme power. Call that power God, or what ever you will. Also, because death is so final, it staggers the mind. There is no debate after the event. There is no chance to reconsider. You can't take it to a higher court to reverse the decision. Death is a total and final cut-off of all communications, and I suspect that there is an end to the decision making process of our being.

That is the shocking part of death: It is so abrupt and conclusive. We try to avoid the contemplation of death. We feel that if we ignore it, it will go away and it won't happen to us. But even if we ignore death until God calls us, eventually the aging of our bodies will force us to consider it. It's interesting to note that in this final hour, some who live until God calls them and they *shed this mortal coil* will die and then live forever.

Still, the lost of a love one is difficult for the survivor. We are all part of mankind, as John Donne must have known when he wrote that when a person dies, part of us dies. Since we are all part of humanity, part of our humanity also dies. Many of us feel the lost more than others. It becomes more personal. We cry for our loss love and ourselves. We tend to abandon the future. *No man is an island...*So, *don't ask, "For whom the bell tolls...it tolls for thee.*—John Donne 1573-1631.

And life goes on. In spite of our skepticism and doubt, we try to look forward to the future. It has been said that yesterday is a dream and tomorrow is a hope and today is a gift and that's why we call it the present. Every day on earth is a gift from God. So today, we can plan for the future. We hope there will be events that will lift us out of our gloom and lift us to new heights if we only believe—the sun will shine tomorrow. *Do you believe*?

Bishop Sheen once wrote a book titled *Life Is Worth Living*. He said that happiness in this life was part of God's plan for every one of us. Happiness the likes of which we could never have dreamed or wildly anticipated with our minute intelligence, if only we could believe. Christ was right when he said, *Oh, ye of little faith*!

I wonder about some definitions: Socrates said that a philosopher is a seeker of the truth. Isn't every one of us a philosopher? A Ph.D. or Doctor of Philosophy is one who has made a contribution to the truth. Shouldn't Christ and Socrates be given a Ph.D.? Of course! But the paper attesting to a degree is not important. It's what you have done for someone else that's important.

Parenthood is a gift from God that forces us to think of somebody else instead of ourselves bringing joy to our lives. Parents are important, especially mothers. Their unselfish love gives them the perfect opportunity to do something for somebody else without any expectations of getting something back. That's what this whole world is about—an opportunity to do something for somebody else. So I think that we can stop feeling sorry for ourselves if we can do something for somebody else—quick. And it is best if that somebody never finds out who did it. God knows—I'm trying!

About the Author

H. G. Arsenault is a retired General Motors Senior Financial Analysis and Financial data base programmer with 36 years service and seven years with Chrysler subsidiary, VPSI, as a Systems Information Director. He lives with his wife Delores in St Clair Shores, Michigan.

Printed in the United States
55504LVS00002B/199-300

9 780595 200177